Diplomatic Incidents

Also by Cherry Denman

The History Puzzle
A Modern Book of Hours
The Little Green Book
Dreamer of Dreams
The QI Annual (The Unrude Bits)

For Children

Wake Up Charlie Dragon
Molly and the Magic Umbrella
Pirates
The Little Peacock's Gift

Diplomatic Incidents

*The Memoirs of an
(Un)diplomatic Wife*

CHERRY DENMAN

JOHN MURRAY

For Oliver Shilling –
Battler against the Odds

First published in Great Britain in 2010 by John Murray (Publishers)
An Hachette UK Company

2

A CIP catalogue record for this title is available from the British Library

ISBN 978-1-84854-241-9

Typeset in Monotype Fournier by Servis Filmsetting Ltd, Stockport, Cheshire

Printed and bound by Clays Ltd, St Ives plc

John Murray policy is to use papers that are natural, renewable and recyclable products and
made from wood grown in sustainable forests. The logging and manufacturing processes are
expected to conform to the environmental regulations of the country of origin.

John Murray (Publishers)
338 Euston Road
London NW1 3BH

www.johnmurray.co.uk

Contents

Contents

List of Main Illustrations

Things I've Learnt Abroad

I

The Beginning

Abroad is bloody.

(George VI)

I am not an enthusiastic traveller.

Abroad means dodgy lavatories and pillows dribbled on by other people. It means taxi drivers in string vests and baby-faced policemen with guns. It's hard work, and it's sweaty and uncomfortable. It is a mystery to me that I appear to have spent rather a lot of my life living on foreign shores. When the world is full of people longing to explore the most revolting corners of the earth and to discover the unexpected, why am I the one who has ended up far-flung and fainthearted in some foreign field?

I am definitely not Suitable Material.

Many years ago, in a moment of absent-minded self-indulgence, I married a diplomat. I still haven't made up my mind whether this was a good move or not. I have turned from a happy, stay-at-home children's book illustrator into a chaotic nomad. My brain seems to be permanently locked in a suitcase, my children are lost somewhere in transit and the husband might as well have 'Heavy Baggage' tattooed somewhere on his person. We all spend far too much time in the air. We don't so much have a carbon footprint, as a carbon cowpat.

I love Sunday newspapers and rain, orderly queues and pork pies. I told my daughter that when I die I want my ashes to be sprinkled all the way up the King's Road, a pinch in all my favourite haunts and the final smidgeon lightly dusted on the top of a cappuccino at Oriel's. She was very unsympathetic: 'You can rot down to compost like everybody else.' Anyone would have thought that I had asked her to drink it.

I can think of nothing nicer than being able to live in London. It works; it is beautiful. We speak the same language. We laugh at the same things; the clothes are my size and I can buy lavatory paper 365 days of the year. If I feel like it, I can draw a moustache on a picture of the Queen and not be beheaded.

This is a Good Thing.

Baden-Powell's book *Rovering to Success* talks about navigating one's canoe through the rapids of life. I know

what he means. I have rammed rocks, lost my paddle and gone up the wrong creek entirely. I cannot pretend to offer you the Baden-Powell guide to life abroad, but I have made the same mistakes so often that I can now dimly recognize them. I pass them on, not so that you can avoid them – you won't – but in order to offer you some companionship when you pick yourself up from the wreckage of cultural collision.

I have never really seen the point of travel, despite having run up more air miles than a Kenyan French bean. I treat aeroplanes like buses and Heathrow like my downstairs loo – get in and out as quickly as possible, but arm yourself with the *Times* crossword in case it takes longer than anticipated.

Reluctant travellers like me are easy to spot at Heathrow. On landing we lick the tarmac, we smile at BAA staff in Terminal 5, we dry-hump the *Country Life* stack at WH Smith. Every time my plane descends out of the clouds over southern England I look out of the window and get a lump in my throat. Green fields buttered and buffed, fluffy hedgerows, flint and brick cottages with Samuel Palmer smoking chimney-stacks. I swear that I once saw Postman Pat. On returning from one long stint abroad and hearing the nasal, flat-toned voice of the British Airways pilot (why are they always called Tim or Nigel?) welcoming us all 'back home', I was reduced to chin-quivering sobs. I was still blubbing as I wheeled my squeaking trolley through Nothing to Declare.

Yet with the relief of return comes a strange sense of not belonging, a desperate new-girl-at-school desire to fit in and be one of the gang again. I remember after three years in mid-1980s Peking accompanying my much-loved and ever elegant sister-in-law to Sainsbury's. Unused to such a profusion of products I cooed and gasped. 'Shut up,' she hissed. 'Everyone will think you've just been let out of prison.' Chastened, I filled two enormous trolleys with goodies, forgetting that, unlike in communist concrete heaven, everything would still be available the following week.

Living abroad changes you; it marks you out. We don't look right or sound the same. When I fly back, it takes days for me to get back up to speed with my friends, who never know what I am talking about. I sometimes do not know what they are on about either. But at least I am not as bad as my husband Charlie, who on return from China found himself sitting next to a well-known actress at a dinner party.

'What do you do?' he asked.

'Oh, I'm just an actress,' she said, tossing her hair and smouldering.

'How exciting. Have you been in anything I have heard of?'

'A little thing called *EastEnders*.' A horrible silence followed and I knew what was coming.

'No, never heard of it. Have you been in anything else?'

The thesp deflated. I later found out she had rather a large part.

It is our fault. While we are away we are in a timewarp. We have changed but home stays the same. Natasha Wilson, the wife of the ex-governor of Hong Kong, once said to me: 'At first you resent your friends for never changing. But later you resent them if they do.' We want to remain part of the tribe, but we have become uncertain about some of the rituals.

For example, we look different. We have a tan in mid-winter, which friends don't find endearing. I have usually brought all the wrong clothes and completely forgotten all footwear except for one left shoe. I find myself on the tube wearing clothes which are fine in the sunshine of abroad, but in rainy, grey, sophisticated London make me look like the mad aunt whom nobody wants to ask for Christmas.

And we *are* different. Travelling on a short holiday is a great adventure, but you know that you will return to clean sheets and a choice of shampoos. But *living* abroad stamps us earth-wanderers with the Mark of Cain. It is altogether different making a home in a strange place; knowing that your life, your children's lives and your heart are now part of it; that your happiness depends on you making it work. It is hard. It is exhilarating and I am gloriously bad at it.

What keeps me going are the crowds of slightly lost, homesick, wonderful women I have found wherever I have ended up. Each one is creating her own small version of her homeland around her and wearing it like a protective snail-shell, trying to make the puzzles of everyday a little easier to cope with. The simple cry of 'Does anyone know where to buy loo paper?' can bond a group of women in a matter of seconds.

Tears and plate-throwing, especially at the start, are normal. In fact, being faintly miserable when you arrive in a strange place makes you much more approachable than

being relentlessly upbeat. There is more of a 'quick fag behind the bike shed' feeling of camaraderie between women who want to wallow in a moan, and nothing more nauseating than someone who thinks it is all simply wonderful. Especially on a morning when the sewers have just backed up, the electricity has gone off and you have found a cockroach the size of a guinea-pig in your sink. So pitch it right: miserable, but not too miserable; cheerful, but not too cheerful. Easy once you get the hang of it. Of course, in front of your husband, or Officially Recognized Partner, as the Foreign Office like to title those not bound in holy matrimony (ORP – how romantic) you must be as miserable as you possibly can, because he is the bastard who brought you to this god-forsaken hole.

Every time I move countries I make mistakes: I am either too loud and too pushy, or too unfriendly and too reserved. It is impossible to get it right: the only thing to remember is that everyone gets it wrong. It takes weeks to settle in and no one should judge you until you have lived there for at least a year. If you are still a grumpy old goat after that, then they have every right to exclude you from their lives.

Living abroad is very humbling. Being in someone else's country is a great leveller, especially if you do not speak their language. I am living proof that you need a talent to learn languages. Abroad I am in effect dumb and illiterate. I have to rely on my talent for mime and my ability to make a complete fool of myself in front of complete strangers. I am still proud of my impersonations at my local halal butcher in Tripoli, when attempting to buy duck, geese or turkey for Christmas dinner. Actually, camel made a nice change.

It is also shaming to see how welcoming and polite most people abroad are. Shop-owners press free chocolate bars on you and leap up to shake your hand. Your children are petted and spoiled, and complete strangers carry your shopping home for you. I have been rugby-tackled into people's homes, had tea forced upon me and been treated like royalty. 'For God's sake,' I want to cry, 'I could be a mad, axe-wielding psycho. I might eat your children, empty your fridge and steal your copies of *National Geographic*. Why are you welcoming me into your house?' Arab hospitality in particular is eye-watering. You have to be careful not to admire their clothes too effusively in case they whip them off their backs and give them to you.

Abroad, you become beguiled by the kindness of strangers and do things you would never dream of doing at home. In Borneo I once visited an open-air museum, one of those places where whole villages are reconstructed so that you can see how people lived in their longhouses. At the ticket office I handed over my backpack, umbrella and infant son. About an hour later it nibbled faintly at my conscience. Leaving your son at the hat-and-coat drop of a museum in England would lead to a visit from the social

services. Rushing back to the entrance I found that ticket sales had plummeted while the entire staff amused my baby. They were rather put out when I suggested that he should be with his mother for the rest of the afternoon. Abashed, I handed over his bottle and a nappy and continued the tour (can't see that happening in Madame Tussaud's).

I have moved around the world for twenty-five years now and I still cry for three months every time I arrive in a new place. Yet I would not have missed a single day, left out a single experience or not met a single person. Every bizarre incident and every strange accident broadens your heart in a way that living safely and comfortably can never do. I pride myself in always failing to learn from my mistakes because it is through howlers that adventures develop; being in the wrong place at the wrong time is the only way to live. As George Foreman said: 'The most horrifying thing in the world is to be without an adventure.'

George, you are so right.

2
Arrivals and Departures

Great God! This is an awful place!
(Robert Falcon Scott)

*How to move abroad without losing your passport,
marbles or husband*

PACKING UP

Apparently moving house and divorce are two of the most stressful things a person can experience in their lifetime. Personally, I find the two invariably go together.

Every time I have to pack up and move on and my brain becomes clogged with dreary concerns like mattress-protectors and meter-readings, I find myself more preoccupied with planning my decree nisi than the packing order. And as the move progresses and I watch with mounting misery the chunks of my happy life dismantled around me, I find my thoughts turn more to dismemberment and disembowelling rather than the softer option of divorce. Forget a pound of flesh: I want to see viscera. A long prison sentence – fifteen years in the same place – seems remarkably tempting, as I try to pack up the kitchen knives without first using them on Charlie. Husbands, take note. When moving house, never sneak up behind your wives in the kitchen; you never know what she might be holding in her clenched fist.

Ripping out the entrails of your life and stuffing them into boxes is always horrible. You will never get used to it. The only benefit of having to move so often is that it stops you drowning in your own rubbish. I have come to look on it as a sort of domestic colonic irrigation, a purging of the layers of detritus festering all over my house and which become such a health hazard that I have to check the removal men are up to date with their tetanus jabs.

There are only two golden rules when packing up. The first concerns storage. STORAGE IS FOR SUCKERS. You would do better to stuff everything on eBay and put the money towards a top-notch divorce lawyer.

The second golden rule is the P Principle: preliminary, preventative packing precautions. This may sound like one of those management courses delivered by those who

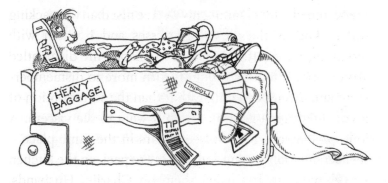

can't to those who have to, but is far more important. Before the packers arrive put all your passports, mobile phones, house keys, car keys, wallets and household pets in a box and lodge them with your next-door neighbour. Otherwise I guarantee that, as you wave goodbye to the removal lorry, you will hear your mobile trilling merrily – or, worse still, the familiar alarmed squeak of your daughter's guinea-pig – from somewhere deep within.

Until that lorry disappears from outside your front door, it is a bit like having a baby – your life is completely out of your control. I recommend a very strong alcoholic epidural, not least because you won't be able to take any of your old stash with you. Sitting on the floor in your empty house, getting gently sozzled on a cocktail of Drambuie and the Malibu your cleaning lady gave you for Christmas, is as good a way to go as any.

Packers are genetically programmed to pack anything/ everything, so it is best to limit them to one or two rooms, in which you have pre-positioned only the things you want to take with you and NOT the things which are staying. Unpacking crockery in Hong Kong, I came across a pile of smelly plates covered in green fur. I was mystified until I realized that the packers had simply swept up all our dirty breakfast things before I'd had time to wash them up. Eggs, bacon and mushrooms look very different after eight weeks on the high seas.

ARRIVING

Our first posting was to the still very Communist China in the early 1980s, when Tiananmen Square was still tank-free and Deng was more than just a fertilizer. We had not been married very long, so not only was there a completely new country and civilization to deal with, but, previously in control of career and self, it was the first time I had been a 'wife'. My only reason for being in the soldier, worker, peasant paradise was to accompany Charlie: overnight I felt as if the word 'appendage' had been tattooed on my forehead. Anyone who has seen *Lost in Translation* will recognize that emptiness of being alone in a foreign country when your husband or wife goes off for their first day at work. It always takes a few months of marking territory and renegotiating borders before the status quo is re-established. Even so, after twenty-five years the feeling of trotting behind your husband on a lead never quite goes away.

No matter how thrilled you may be at your posting, homesickness almost invariably raises its hideous head at some time or another. For me, the only cure is my girlfriends, who ring to tell me that life at home is really dull, that the weather is awful, the dog has fleas, and they have gone up two dress sizes since Christmas. Warn your friends in advance not to bang on about what a wonderful time they are having. I once cried for two days on hearing about a particularly exciting school cricket match that I had missed. But they get you through those first bewildering weeks and out the other side ready to fight the next battle.

Actually, China remains to this day my favourite posting. Every day brought something unexpected. Being sent to tough places, as it was then, is often more fun than the easy options, because everyone mucks in. And the friendships you forge in tricky times are often those that last the longest.

HOUSE-HUNTING

Finding the right place to live is the key to being happy in a posting abroad. Find the right bunker and you can face any assault. You may have to make yourself unpopular in the fight to find the right home, but remember that people love it when you behave badly on first arrival: it brightens their day and gives them something juicy to talk about.

Not that we had any choice as to where we lived in China. In the 1980s every foreigner had to live in one of two diplomatic compounds consisting of hideous tower-blocks crammed into a walled, treeless and well-guarded enclosure. Comings and goings were carefully monitored and restricted. Once, in the deafening explosion of rockets and firecrackers which welcome in the Chinese New Year, a stray firework smashed through the seventh-floor window of an absent embassy colleague, back in England for his mid-tour leave, and set it on fire. The fire engine was called, but the guards refused to allow it entry into the diplomatic compound because it couldn't show a written invitation ('The First Secretary of the British Embassy and his wife, Nigel and Amaryllis Boggis Rolfe, invite you to the burning of their flat at 21:30. Dress formal. RSVP'). The diplomatic corps rallied round with buckets of water; the journalists rushed for their cameras and type-writers.

The Chinese authorities considered foreigners rather unwelcome necessities in the 1980s, like flu-jabs or worm-pills. I remember coming back to our flat one afternoon to find two Chinese men sitting on the sofa, reading my magazines with their feet up on the coffee table. Above their heads the wall lights had been disconnected and wiring poked out from two holes in the wall. When I asked them what they were doing, they told me that they were fixing the television aerial. We did not have a television at that time, but who was I to argue? If ever there was a fault in the flat, I simply complained to the wall and someone came round to fix it.

We got used to it. Romania in the bad old days of the Ceauşescus sounded far worse. Two American friends told me that every time they had guests for a meal they would be woken up at four o'clock in the morning by the ringing of their bedside telephone. When they picked it up, they could hear a recording of their own dinner party. They tried taking the phone off the hook, but the recording came anyway, the only difference being that the phone didn't ring first. Another colleague had just arrived in Bucharest without his wife. He is very short-sighted. Sitting in his bath, he heard the phone ring. Among the soapsuds he could not find his glasses. Someone handed him the phone. Only after he had taken the call did he remember that he was meant to be alone in the flat.

As there was only one flat available in Peking I had to take it without a fuss. In Hong Kong and Cyprus I was able to choose our new house. In Libya we found ourselves having to take over the house of our predecessor. He was a lovely man but apparently lacked any sense of smell. Libyans believe in filling their plot of land right up to the outside walls, and running all along the rear of the house, two feet from all the bedroom and kitchen windows, was a small but absolutely humming goat farm.

Skins and hooves of previous inmates were piled high (in both senses) on the corrugated iron goat-shed roofs, along with old rubber tyres, rusty buckets and an ominously stained mattress. An area half the size of a tennis court was home to thirty goats, a flock of chickens, half a dozen rabbits, three mangy stray cats and two Alsatian puppies, who howled disconsolately at every call to prayer and then barked happily all night. Did you know that goats snore? They also cough, sneeze, wheeze, talk in their sleep and fart. The goats began to take over our lives. Have you ever smelt goat's cheese close up? Not just close, but sleeping in your bed and borrowing your underwear? I would fling open the windows on warm sunny

days only to be knocked back by a wall of flies and a smell which you could have made mulligatawny from. I have a teenage son, who wears trainers in bed and thinks that showers are for boys who sing in the church choir, so my threshold is quite high. But this smell crept in under the doors and made our tea taste funny.

In the end we persuaded the embassy to move us upwind on the grounds that we could entertain goats or work contacts, but not both. There are some nights when I miss the whole Whipsnade experience: the bleating, the caterwauling, the howling; the dawn chorus from the two cockerels, whom we named Sarkozy and de Villepin because of their competitive crowing, and the happy herds

de Villepin
&
Sarkozy

of blowflies grazing on my breakfast . . . but on the whole, I'm much happier.

In Cyprus we had a teacher friend who lived in a remote cottage on the Turkish side. He became friendly with the local doctor, an old man, who confided in him that during his early years as the village GP he had spent an alarming amount of time dissuading the male populace from mounting their donkeys. Our friend thought that this was a huge joke and returned the confidence by saying that in the more rural areas of Britain it was rumoured that farmers preferred sheep to their wives. On hearing this, the doctor rose, his face stony with horror, and said that that was the most disgusting thing he had ever heard. To this day Robin has no idea why such offence was taken. Was it a misunderstanding? Is the Turkish word for 'sheep' similar to the one for 'much-loved old aunt', or is it because a donkey is considered one of the family, whereas sheep are lunch? Given that one of Robin's students was called Ufuk Dedmen, he presumed that the Turks would be a little more robust about such matters.

Our house in Cyprus was another huge cement-block bunker. Public lavvy on the outside and a cross between a French brothel and a mausoleum on the inside. It had a beautiful, big garden full of orange and lemon trees, from which we made buckets of the most delicious, black sticky marmalade. In the sun everything grew: great scarlet

HOW TO MAKE
·BLACK·
~ MARMALADE ~

2 Kg Seville oranges (approx 8/9)
3 lemons
1 sweet orange
1 grapefruit
7½ pints water
2 Kg preserving sugar
700g dark brown sugar
1 dessertspoon of black treacle

Wash all the fruit thoroughly.
Put it in a large pan with the water & cover.
Bring to the boil and cook over low heat for
1½ hours or until the fruit pierces easily.
Lift out the fruit & cool.
Cut the fruit in half and scoop
out all the insides & pips which you put
back into the cooking liquid.

Chop the peel into the size you like.
Boil the liquid & insides for about 20/30
minutes until reduced by almost half.
Strain the liquid into a HUGE saucepan,
add the chopped peel, the 2 sugars &
the treacle.

Boil until set, then cool and put in jars.

*FOR THOSE WHO LIKE A LITTLE BACKBONE
WITH THEIR BREAKFAST.*

geraniums, roses and a huge hedge of fresh basil, which kept us in pesto sauce all year and blew its peppery scent through the house every evening, catching the breeze and filling each room with the smell of summer.

We bought a trampoline and an enormous blow-up swimming pool which squatted malignantly on my lawn all year for all the world like a huge blue breast implant. The children revised for their exams in it. We never got the hang of chlorine tablets, and by the end of summer with all the olives plopping in from the overhanging branches, the water turned into a black, bubbling stew.

The only problem with our house in Cyprus was that when it rained in that spectacular Mediterranean down-pour way, the rainwater coursed down the street and took a right turn directly into our garage and basement. One afternoon we returned from the airport having picked up the children, only to find the basement under three feet of grey, greasy water. We promptly called out the Nicosia fire brigade, who arrived wearing incredibly smart uniforms and shiny dress shoes. Clearly they had no intention of ruining their smart, new footwear by getting them wet. Sighing, they told us that there wasn't enough depth of water to justify the use of the pump on their throbbing new fire engine. Our Cypriot neighbour came up with the solution: 'So add more water,' he suggested helpfully.

The firemen shrugged and waved sweetly as they drove away, leaving us to do things the old-fashioned way.

Unfortunately the water had got into the store-room where we had neatly piled all the cardboard boxes from our move. If you have ever seen a large room filled with warm, gloopy porridge, you will know how much fun that was to clean up. I didn't know whether to use a mop or a spoon.

SETTLING IN

Our children have always been a bit wary of new houses. The first afternoon of Barnaby's first holiday in Nicosia I sent him down the road to buy a loaf from the bakery. He came back round-eyed and shell-shocked, declaring that we had rented a house in a really 'dodgy' area: the bakery was full of transvestites. This was an understandable mistake: many of the local ladies did apply their make-up with a trowel and most of them sported the scariest fake bosoms I have ever seen. I also had to explain to my thirteen-year-old son all about the Mediterranean 'hair belt' and that a five o'clock shadow was quite normal on women here. Indeed every time I went for a leg wax they asked me if I wanted my facial hair strimmed at the same time. Poor Freddie, my blonde and beautiful daughter, experienced a Cypriot leg wax and had to jump all the way home after the waxer went far too far up and her butt cheeks got glued together.

The easiest way to settle in quickly is to meet as many people as possible in as short a time as possible. Say

'yes' to every single offer that comes your way. This will inevitably lead to a few nightmare situations, but the whole point of being abroad is that you do things that you would not dream of doing at home.

Language lessons, tennis, book clubs, bridge, amateur dramatics – you should sign up for every single one. You may then have to spend the next few years trying desperately to get out of them, as your passion for naked Ukrainian folk dancing or Mongolian grunt songs wanes somewhat, but you will have met loads of new and exciting people, and naked Ukrainians are a sure-fire way of livening up boring dinner parties.

Learning the language is, of course, hugely important, although I have failed miserably in every country in which we have ever lived. In Mandarin all I could say was: 'And how many children do you have? Oh, one . . . really.' And: 'No, no. Green suits you.' When what I really wanted to say was: 'Frankly, I would rather eat my own face than stick that greasy, grey turtle testicle in my mouth.' And: 'I don't care if it did cost 2,000 yuan a kilo: eating something that is still breathing and well enough to rollerskate is plain wrong.' That was on the occasion when our hosts served live lobster. Its flesh had been cut off and laid on top of its still-moving body. It tasted delicious, but like the eyes of Kitchener in the poster, that lobster watched my every move.

My Mandarin teacher would become so bored with my inability to grasp a single grammatical rudiment that halfway through each lesson she would close her folder and say, 'So, Cherry, may I ask you a personal question?' These ranged from the bizarre to the eye-wateringly intimate. One of my favourites was: 'So, Cherry, are many people in England named after fruit and vegetables?' And then there was the baffling: 'So, Cherry, if you are at a party, how do you explain to the host that you need to defecate?'

In Hong Kong, my Cantonese teacher gave up on me completely and instead took it upon herself to educate me in all things Hong Kong Chinese. Our first outing was to a Canto-porn film called *Sex and Zen*, which had one of the most hilarious scenes I have ever seen, involving a fourteenth-century apothecary, a horse's penis, a transplant and a thunderstorm. The cinema was full of little old Chinese ladies, who had brought along picnics and cackled their way through the entire film, screaming with laughter at all the rude bits. 'Ah, Chinese hot dog!' called out one sweet old dear, as the hero's member was wrapped in warm bread.

She also introduced me to Jackie Chan's early Kung Fu films, Cantonese gossip magazines ('she's the richest girl in China, but she's been locked away for eating her own baby') and some of the best dim sum I have ever eaten. My Chinese grammar remained non-existent, but I was the only student who enjoyed her homework.

Mind you, being able to speak the language can sometimes get you into more trouble than you might realize. A friend in the embassy who spoke Chinese came home for lunch wearing a brand-new three-piece suit. As he stepped out of the lift to his diplomatic compound flat, he saw that a Chinese worker was spray-painting the hall outside. He merrily quipped to the painter in Mandarin that it was a good thing that he could speak Chinese so that he could warn him not to turn round and spray his new, smart suit. The painter, amazed to hear a 'Big Nose' speaking fluent Chinese, turned round to have a good look, thereby coating Tony from the top of his head to his shiny shoes in white emulsion.

WALKING

Another way to learn your way around a new place is to go walking. In Libya this was particularly important because there are no street names and no house numbers; knowing where you were was the only option. The trouble was that all the houses looked pretty much the same and familiar landmarks tended to be demolished overnight in order to make way for the Great Development Project. Unfortunately the Libyans are better at demolishing than building, so most of Tripoli looks like a bombsite, which, of course, it is every decade or so, courtesy of the Americans.

I found the best way to start was to begin with a circle of one block around your house and then extend your range by a block every time you go out. The only danger is that many large cities in the developing world have not been designed for pedestrians: there are no pavements, or, if they do exist, they are for dumping rubbish and parking cars. Prepare to scramble.

TAXIS

Braving local taxis combines getting to know your way around with learning the local language. Most foreign taxi drivers are immensely jolly. They think it is a hoot to have a mad English woman in the back, massacring their language and paying over the odds. It is, of course, essential to have a good grounding in charades: miming 'Ministry of Foreign Affairs' is a lot harder than *Oliver Twist*, I can tell you.

From your taxi driver you will also learn all the local hand-gestures, as well as those short, pithy aphorisms which can come in so handy at diplomatic functions.

I once got stuck with a taxi driver in Tripoli, who, like most of his colleagues, drove at a hundred miles an hour while steering with one finger. Turning right round, he yelled at me, 'Music?'

'Fine,' I replied, clinging on to the back seat for dear life.

'Fuck you,' came back the ungracious reply.

'No, really. It's fine.'

'Fuck you,' he insisted. This went on for a good few minutes as we weaved erratically between cars until he finally slotted in the tape and I realized that it was the title track on a very unpleasant American rap album, which he obviously treasured.

When we finally arrived and I emerged from the cab wobble-kneed and teeth clenched, I had the great pleasure of pointing to his tape deck: 'Fuck you,' I said, beaming.

LEAVING AND PACKING UP AGAIN

Of course, with all the chaos of arriving and leaving, of packing and unpacking and repacking, of saying good-byes and hellos, the thing to avoid at all costs is the humiliation of leaving something behind.

HAND GESTURES
TO BE AVOIDED
ABROAD

GREECE

THE MOUTZA
"I'm not listening."

ITALY

"You have a face a bit like a lady's bottom.'"

ASIA

"Go and procreate."

THE MIDDLE EAST AND MOST OF THE EDGWARE ROAD

"Go stick your nose up a camel's bottom."

THE FULL ENGLISH

"Please leave the vicinity quite quickly."

WORLDWIDE

"Your member has moved north."

EUROPE & AMERICA

"I don't think so."

KOREA

"You are a dog."

BRAZIL

"Arsehole.."

THE PHILIPPINES

"Your mother is a dog."

SPAIN & PORUGAL

"Guess what your wife is doing with the milkman."

INDIA

"I care little for your opinion."

When we left our flat in Peking and went to the management officer to sign off, he told us round-eyed and whispering that when doing the last check he had found something 'quite horrible' under the bed. Charlie and I spent our last two nights in a hotel sleepless and racking our brains trying to guess what it could be. A used pink, fluffy condom with go-faster stripes and spoilers, maybe? A copy of *Choirboy Monthly*? Unable to stand it a moment longer, we went back and demanded to know.

It was a two-and-a-half-inch cockroach. Hell, I cuddled up with those every night; we were on first-name terms. How sweet of him to think that I kept the flat so clean that we had no wildlife cohabiting with us. The roaches in our house had their own keys. Two sleepless nights just for a cockroach.

On leaving Nicosia for Tripoli we had forgotten to empty out one high, dusty old bedroom cupboard. Three weeks after we arrived in Libya we received a gleeful email from our successors in Cyprus. It read: 'Have found your lederhosen. Am forwarding them by first available diplomatic bag.' He had copied the message to most of the office.

Bastard.

3
Transport Abroad

In Milan, traffic lights are instructions. In Rome they are suggestions. In Naples, they are Christmas decorations.
(Antonio Martino)

How to get to the end of the world and back in one piece

CARS, CRASHES AND CLUTZ CONTROL

If you see a car coming very fast towards you on the wrong side of the motorway with the contents of a large house including the kitchen sink piled on the roof and with various breeds of livestock taking up room on the passenger seats, then the chances are that you are not in Surrey.

Every country breeds the drivers it deserves and by observing its driving habits you can probe deeply into that nation's psyche. In Britain we yearn to emulate the 'Eat My Dust' laddishness of *Top Gear*. Yet when it comes down to it, our revved-up, high-octane, throbbing menfolk drive off to their mum's for Sunday lunch with all the pent-up aggression of nuns coming back from Easter mass with a tray of eggs on the back seat of their Morris Minor. We cannot forget that we are the race which spawned the Scout movement and we drive with all the care and attention of a Brown Owl cleaning a Brownie's grazed knee.

Observe, if you will, the behaviour of local drivers at any really busy junction in any city in the world, but preferably one with traffic lights, and you will see the inner workings of a country's brain. Imagine the cars are nerve pulses, little four-door hatchback action potentials zipping round the neural pathways of the city's cerebral cortex, getting stuck at the lights, sneaking off left to a side-street synapse, only to discover that some bastard has double-parked, can't reverse, boxed in – boom! – blood-clot on the brain.

Each city has its own mental health problems. Cairo has been completely paralysed for years due to a stroke-inducing aneurysm in down-town Azbakiya. Calcutta has restricted movement having been crippled by multiple pile-up sclerosis. Zurich and Berlin have galloping OCD, while Rome suffers from paranoid schizophrenia due to Roman men being forced to drive tiny Smart cars; the only make small enough to zip down all the tiny alley-ways. Fine little foetus cars, but hardly macho enough for an Italian male with his furry testicles dangling from the rear-view mirror. Cyprus has early-onset Alzheimer's: Cypriot drivers forget which lane they are meant to be in and then dribble to a halt in the fast lane, clutching their mobile phones to their ears.

Tripoli, however, is in the throes of a full-on psychotic breakdown. I have never seen such appalling driving as in Libya. In Beirut they drive as if they have rockets up their bottoms, which sometimes they do, but at least *can* drive.

In Libya they just *think* they can drive, which is an entirely different thing. Lane discipline is a concept they have never grasped. These normally jovial, beautifully mannered people turn into demons from the depths of hell when they slide behind the wheel.

And it's not just car drivers. I watched in horror one day as a young disabled man on a decrepit motorized invalid tricycle crazily gunned his way around one of the three most dangerous roundabouts in North Africa. (Known by the foreigners variously as Death Roundabout, Malfunction Junction and Suicide Circle, these roundabouts are basically Indie car circuits, but faster and without the good manners.) With black smoke pouring out of his exhaust pipe, his hair streaming out behind him and his mouth open in a Banzai scream, he swerved in and out of the speeding cars. He was certainly going to get either to the other side or to the Other Side. Or maybe he had just made a big mistake on his way to the local corner shop. Either way, respect was in order.

Bicycles and Libya do not mix. Not even Charlie, who is a fully paid-up member of the Militant Cycling Tendency when in London, would dare to take his life into his hands in Libya.

Tripoli is dangerous because, unlike other cities which are overcrowded and where the traffic has to crawl, the locals can exercise their automobilistic lunacy at speed. I have seen a man driving round a roundabout the wrong

Well done everybody..... well done.

THE
MILITARY
ATTACHÉ

way, which given the angle of the slip roads was a feat of perversity; another driving his BMW with a baby in one hand and the steering wheel in the other; and a family being transported in the claw of a digger. Going the wrong way up a dual carriageway is standard. And then there are the pedestrians. There are few protected places for people to cross the road, so on the three-lane highway which runs along the seafront people just have to take their lives into their hands and dodge. It is known locally as the 'inshallah shuffle'.

If there is a crash everyone stops and gawps, so both sides of the motorways are frequently blocked as people cross to get a better look. Testament to the appalling driving is to be found about twenty miles to the west of Tripoli on the way to Tunisia. There is situated the world's largest car graveyard cum second-hand shop. Mile after mile after mile of smashed cars of every make and colour known to man have been piled together. A monstrous mausoleum of mangled machines; twisted bonnets, dented wings, crumpled boots. Cars that have rolled or slithered under lorries, cars that no longer resemble anything you could actually sit in. The mind reels thinking about all the death, injury and maiming that has gone into the creation of this monument to folly. I once saw a broken windscreen shattered into little squares of pixilated glass with the shape of a face easily recognizable. You could even see the nose.

It is a giant second-hand parts market. The cars are arranged by make and model, so that if you need, for example, to replace the back rear wing of a Volvo, you head for the Volvo section and find a car of the same model and make. Bargain with the man in charge, wipe off the blood and bolt it on. And if you make it through next week, you can come back for a new door. When everything salvageable has been removed from a car, the empty chassis are piled up into great mountainous walls. Huge bastions of multicoloured car corpses form rusted, jagged battlements, a haunting reminder of the fatalism of the Arab mind.

Whereas Libyan driving is in a class of its own, Cyprus boasts the highest rate of road deaths in the European Union. Hong Kong, however, was like a police state, so everyone behaved. China *was* a police state. Not that you would have guessed. The use of the rear-view mirror must have been considered revisionist behaviour; perhaps indicating was making a leftist or rightist political statement and that is why no one ever did. This was the country, which, during the Cultural Revolution, changed the green and red lights on the traffic signals so that red meant 'go'. After all you could not have the colour of the Great People's Revolution meaning 'stop'. And despite the few cars on the road, they still had an impressive hit rate. I once saw five fatal accidents on a 100-mile stretch of new fast road. No wonder the English language *Peking*

Daily boasted of progress in road-making: 'China now has 400 km of high-speed dual carnage way.'

But no matter how bad or dangerous the driving abroad, to have complete freedom in a country you have to join in the demolition Derby. Some people hire a driver, but would you really want to entrust your life to someone with whom you wouldn't share a car at the dodgems? For the first few times on the road, I'd recommend starting when few others are around. In Arab countries this means on a Friday, in less-civilized countries during the World Cup or a national football match. Stay in the slow lane. Keep calm. Watch every mirror like a hawk. Ignore the fact that the cars coming towards you look as if they are part of the Royal Artillery Motorcycle Display team. Like you, they are probably just manoeuvring around potholes.

You will have to accept the fact that if you drive abroad your car will get trashed, which is a good reason to buy one that is not too smart in the first place. If the local Lewis Hamilton does not get you, then the climate or wildlife will. My friend Ernst Zimmerman was nearly wiped out by mating bullfrogs. He was coming back from a picnic in the mountains outside Peking one evening when he came round a corner and found the road completely covered in amphibians in flagrante. It was not a case of moving them out of the way or swerving round them: they were a solid humping mass. There

was not much point in slowing down either. After all from a bullfrog's point of view a ton of Mercedes on your back is going to render you two-dimensional whatever speed it is doing. Ernst did his best to avoid them, but he said that it was like driving over footballs filled with custard.

Then there is the servicing problem. Abroad is either very hot or very cold, or sandy or muddy. Until recently the Foreign Office insisted that their staff had to buy cars made in the UK. Fine, until you have to get spare parts. In China we had to drive around for three months with the driver's side of the windscreen smashed, while a replacement was sent out. It was all right as long as you leant to the left, but when the new one arrived, it took me a while to get used to sitting upright again. British cars are not built for minus thirty or plus fifty. But we did find a good use for the awful cheap vodka that in those days Bulgarians or Russians gave as presents. We put it in the windscreen-washer reserve to stop it freezing.

Language difficulties only increase the problems of servicing. Poor Kay Smith took her car for a straightforward service and mistook the Chinese words for 'stop' and 'go'. With great dignity and at slow speed she drove her car nose first into the repair pit. Luckily it was empty at the time. Mary, a friend in Hong Kong, destroyed her car in pursuit of beauty: she drove into a bollard on the harbour front whilst looking admiringly at a French sailor.

At the end of your time abroad you have the awful problem of what to do with a distressed, dented and frog-splattered car. Like us, you will probably end up bringing it back to the UK.

Actually, it is rather liberating driving around London with the scars of foreign battles. BMWs treat you with respect. No one cuts you up when they know that trading scrapes means nothing to you. On school sports days, our bashed-up, old imported car squatted like a filthy rescue dog next to all the pedigree four-by-fours in the car park. The masters at Barnaby's school christened it the 'Stinkmobile', after an unfortunate accident involving a tray of eggs on the back seat and an emergency stop. The smell seeped behind the radio and into the gearbox, and even years later a sharp left turn would result in a sulphurous stench, followed by passionate denials from all the passengers.

The Stinkmobile was much loved. An ancient Vauxhall Cavalier, it had a radio aerial made from an old coathanger bent into the shape of a heart courtesy of the local garage hands. Most of the upholstery had been replaced by gaffer tape and lichen held the windscreen in place. Muddy rugby boots, cricket teas, lacrosse sticks, pets and hamburger consumption were encouraged. Everyone who hitched a ride had to sign the roof with a permanent marker, which was tied to the driver's headrest.

Once at the end of a very smart London party, I merrily asked if anyone would like a lift home. Across the room a female voice took up my offer and to my horror I found myself face to face with the actress Jacqueline Bisset, dressed from head to toe in white linen. I tried to dissuade her. My car was little more than a dustbin on wheels; you needed a tetanus jab even to open the bonnet. She sweetly said that it was no problem and not only got into the car, but stayed in it chatting for ages after we had found our way to her house in South Kensington. As I watched her retreating figure disappear into the night, three things struck me. Firstly, what a thoroughly charming person she was; secondly, that I had forgotten to ask her to sign the roof; and thirdly, what would she think when she found the old piece of greasy croissant stuck to her left buttock?

Our beloved Stinkmobile finally gave up the ghost one damp Monday morning in London in a full Viking funeral pyre. Charlie accused me of setting it on fire, but he was in Afghanistan at the time. When I discovered the fire I roared to the telephone to call the fire brigade, as I knew the car was full of petrol and that, any minute, crocodiles of children would be walking past on their way to the Montessori school next door.

I dialled 999 and blurted out my name. I tried to explain about the fire, but I was interrupted by a nasal, whining voice calling me 'Madam' (which I hate) and telling me to 'calm down'. As any woman in an excitable state will tell you, being told to calm down, particularly in a patronizing way, has roughly the same effect as shoving a cattle prod up the bottom of a sleeping bull elephant and giving it 4,000 volts of undivided attention.

'I am calm,' I said, calmly.

'No,' said the Linda Snell-like person. (Every word she uttered seemed to abseil straight down from her adenoids.) 'You're still panicking.'

10,000 volts.

'I AM NOT PANICKING.'

'No,' she slimed, 'you're still NOT CALM.'

50,000 volts slammed straight up that bull elephant's back passage. In a voice which would have put the wind up Lord Voldemort I snarled my address and added, 'And you are an annoying, supercilious cow.'

I hung up and sprinted back to the Stinkmobile, which was still committing suttee. After half an hour of dodgy advice from every builder within a two-mile radius, after helpful hints from hundreds of passing schoolboys longing for an explosion and after a lot of tutting from the residents of the nearby old people's home, the fire brigade arrived. But not before my next-door neighbour, back from her school run, had zapped the flames with her kitchen fire extinguisher, so that when the men in yellow rubber finally waddled up, all that was left was a sad pillar of smoke and a faint smell of fried eggs.

The huge fireman surveyed the damage, ran his gimlet eye over the crowd and boomed: 'Which one of you called my controller a supercilious cow?'

'I did,' I said, gimleting him back.

He slapped me on the back. 'You were quite right. Sorry about your car.'

I got the name of a junkyard out of the Yellow Pages and the next day two pock-marked villains like Burke and Hare turned up to take the car away to the knacker's yard. It was all too much for me and as they winched her aboard the tow truck I burst into tears. That old car contained my children's childhood, a wheelbarrowful of memories and terrible smells. I ran back inside and had just poured myself a stiff coffee when the door bell rang. Standing on the steps was either Burke or Hare holding the

number-plates in one hand and the heart-shaped coat-hanger aerial in the other. He handed them to me very graciously with a large tissue.

The Stinkmobile was no more.

BICYCLES

If climate and car culture permit, then I cannot recommend bicycles enough in a foreign posting. Cars are insulating; on a bike you become part of a place, rather than skidding over the surface like a water boatman. There is no better way of exploring a place than with the wind in your hair and a triangle of hardened and pointed leather up your bottom. Bicycles can be fickle, so go for the sturdy variety. One moment they are your solid, reliable friend; the next they have nose-dived into a pothole and you are left with enough gravel in your elbows to furnish a fish-tank.

Sadly, in China nowadays, the car seems to have taken over, but a few years ago the bicycle was king, or Secretary-General, of the Politburo. Stepping off the pavement unexpectedly would cause an explosion of indignant tringling from a million bells, as the solid stream of bicycles would temporarily break and swirl around you like isobars curling around an area of low pressure on a weather map. Zillions of ruddy-cheeked locals in uniform green Mao suits pedalled frantically along on their Flying

Pigeons. My mother-in-law still has one in her garage, which she uses to zip down to the village shops. I swear that if she rear-ended a dumpster, the dumpster would come off worse. Flying Pigeons were designed for the one-child family: mother on the carrier rack and child on the crossbar. Occasionally granny even travelled in a hand-made sidecar. Sometimes the rider was completely obscured by some enormous cargo, so that all you could see was a huge mountain of baskets or watermelons wobbling up the road, seemingly without means of propulsion.

Every bicycle in China had to be licensed and have its own little number-plate bolted on to prove it. We managed to obtain licences for our two normal bicycles, but our trusted tandem, which we had brought out from England, proved more of a problem. It was probably the only one in China at the time and the authorities were instantly suspicious.

First of all they rejected our application because they said that the tandem exceeded the permissible length for a bicycle. Charlie pointed out that it was a tandem not a bicycle. The authorities needed time to consult. On his next visit Charlie argued that it was shorter than two bicycles put end to end and that when mounted the two of us took up less road space than if we had been riding two separate bicycles. 'What if everyone in China rode such a bicycle?' the cadre asked. He could not accept that there might be more space on the roads. The next visit ended with the official claiming that it was illegal for two people to ride one bicycle at the same time. Had he never opened his eyes on the street? All further arguments were met with '*Bu keyi*' or '*Bu xing*' or '*Bu yunxu*' and other variations of 'no'.

So we rode it anyway, without a licence plate. It did rather attract attention. Two Big Noses on a big bike. Occasionally the Peking police spotted our lack of a licence plate. We tried to hide behind the ranks of other cyclists when we rode past a policeman, but at junctions we usually came unstuck, because the traffic cops were raised on a little platform in the middle and got a better view. The pristine white-gloved hands would freeze in the middle of their balletic manoeuvres, the eyes would narrow and then there would be the inevitable sharp blast of the whistle. 'PEDAL LIKE HELL!' would come the order from the captain and we would be off while the traffic policeman leapt on his bike and hared after us. Usually we could burn them off, because a tandem has double the leg-power for the same wind resistance. Sometimes we would deliberately keep just far enough ahead to give the perspiring plod the hope that he might overhaul us and then, when he looked sufficiently red-faced, we would power away. Occasionally we came across an aspiring Christopher Hoy, in which case the game was to make it to the gates of the Foreigners' Compound before being caught, because the policeman was not allowed past the guards without an invitation. Childish, but exciting.

It was also forbidden to park your bike just anywhere in the street. You had to find one of the bike parks policed by an attendant. These parking areas were unimaginably large, crammed with a zillion identical Flying Pigeons balanced precariously on their stands. The only way I could find my bike after shopping was by means of a large pink bow, which I had tied to the handlebars. Strangely no one ever copied my idea.

It was in one of those mega bike parks that I had one of those horribly embarrassing moments which jolt you awake at night. Approaching my beribboned bike, carrying a load of shopping, I tripped on a bike-stand and fell on to my bike, knocking it over on to the next bicycle, which fell on to the next bicycle, which fell on the next bicycle, and so on, for what seemed like an eternity, until the entire 4,000 bicycles had gone down in a bone-crunching game of metal dominoes. I do not know what the parking attendant was screaming at me as I raced past him on my slightly battered bike with its large pink bow, but it did not sound like an uplifting revolutionary slogan.

TRAINS

Without doubt, the best way to make your way to your new posting is by train. If this is impossible, at least try to stop off on the way at as many places as you can, so that you can see how the landscape, the people and the culture change bit by bit as you near your destination. Somehow it softens the edges of difference and eases the change, like tuning a radio very slowly until you finally find your chosen station.

On our first posting we travelled for thirty-six hours in 'Soft Class' from Hong Kong to Peking. Back then, trains in China were divided into two classes: 'Soft Class' for the traveller who insisted upon a few creature comforts, and 'Hard Class' for those of a more stoical disposition. 'Soft Class' consisted of four bunk-beds in a compartment, a dining car and a ratio of one lavatory and basin per thirty passengers; while travelling 'Hard' involved no beds – just wooden benches, a lady who came round twice a day with a tea urn, and a hole in the floor for everyone's bathroom requirements, which, with the usual overcrowding, was approximately one hole for 300 other passengers.

The differences between the two cities in 1985 were still enormous and, despite having watched the gradually changing scenery through the train window, they seemed too big to take in. It was also mid-winter and the temperature was minus fifteen.

Charlie's first steps into China were off the train on to a patch of frozen gob on the platform. Expectoration in China was universal: even Deng Xiaoping had a spittoon by his chair when he met Mrs Thatcher, into which he emitted intermittent projectiles with total accuracy. Charlie's first words as he picked himself up did not quite match those of William the Conqueror as he fell on the beach at Pevensey. His were more Anglo-Saxon.

Our 'let's pretend it's winter' clothes from Hong Kong were woefully inadequate for the harsh wintry conditions in mainland China, and our feet turned to blocks of ice in thirty seconds. In Peking winters if you can bend your arms and legs, then you are not wearing enough layers. In the streets people bounce off each other like padded ping-pong balls, ricocheting down the street, safe and soft and squidgy.

At least on our train journey across China we had managed to travel Soft Class. My poor friend Juliet Hornby had to endure thirty-six hours in Hard Class and arrived in Peking in such a state of culture shock that only a breakfast of hot doughnuts got her back to normal. During the night, having finally dropped off to sleep, she was awoken by a strange, glooping noise, only to open her eyes to see her neighbour enjoying a midnight snack of chicken's brains, which he extracted by holding the chicken above his head and sucking them out through its beak.

We had only been in China a few weeks when my old flatmate Bummer decided to come and stay. It was still mid-winter, grey and icy, but we planned a trip by train to Xian to check out the Terracotta Warriors, just the two of us.

Peking railway station is a great place to introduce visitors to the real China, rather than the one in the travel guides. It is noisy, crammed full of people and chaotic. Everybody shouts. There are families asleep on the floor, people with chickens in their pockets and babies in their backpacks. The whole space smells of tea, garlic, nylon and old socks. There is always a lot of excitement around the escalators: many of the peasants arriving from the countryside have never seen one before, causing pile-ups at the top and bottom like skittles as they hesitate, or fall over at the top.

After navigating the station concourse, Bummer and I discovered we would be sharing our sleeping compartment with an ancient Chinese general and his interpreter. They were both entranced by Bummer as they were convinced that she was Kathy Flowers, at the time the most famous Englishwoman after Margaret Thatcher, known to millions of Chinese because of her English language lessons on television. Apparently Bummer was her exact double. We chatted away happily through the interpreter until

after supper, when both men very sweetly left us alone in the compartment so that we could get ready for bed. We both put on our Laura Ashley nighties (it was the eighties). We later found out the general thought these were evening dresses.

In the morning I woke up and rolled over to see the General opposite, sitting on his bottom bunk looking up at Bummer's bunk with a look of sublime joy on his face. He remained totally immobile and beaming for about ten minutes. Then he sighed and left the compartment. I leapt out of bed to find out what on earth had made him so happy. Bummer's railway blankets had fallen to the floor, her white flannel Laura Ashley special had ridden up above her waist and there, for all the world to see and admire, was her pink, peachy bottom.

From then on the General was her slave. He summoned his eighty-year-old wife, who outrageously had been consigned to Hard Class, to bring his picnic up to the compartment. He then showered Bummer with, rather appropriately, Moon cakes, and thousand-year-old eggs, which were green and slimy and smelled of French lavatories. Having had one of these forced on me too, I hid it up the sleeve of my baggy jumper, where it lurked like a malodorous frog until the awful moment when I had to reach up to my suitcase on the luggage rack. As I raised my arms, it made a break for freedom, slithering up my sleeve and finally coming to rest in the centre of my bra, where it had to stay for three hours until we arrived in Xian. I never did get the smell out of that sweater.

Everyone on the trains was friendly and wanted to practise their English. The exceptions were the harridans who looked after the Soft Class compartments; they were tiny, tough and as mean as snakes. They marched up and down the train corridors in their little white caps and elasticated sleeve-protectors, flinging open the doors, yelling at everybody and turning up the propaganda broadcasts on the compartment radios to full blast. But their most annoying habit was to barge into your compartment in the early morning at least three hours before you were due to arrive at your destination. Peeved that you were still in bed and they were up and working, they would scream that you had to get up and whip away your blanket and pillow before you realized what was going on and could fight back.

But one icy grey dawn, three hours short of Harbin, Charlie found the winning defence. When the dwarfish dragon lady barged in and switched on the lights, we all frantically grabbed at our blankets, only to have them whipped from under our chins with the ruthlessness of an Irish nun. All except Charlie. Dragon lady grabbed his blankets and wrist-whipped them towards her. Charlie

pulled back. She tugged again and Charlie wrenched them back out of her hands. Her shrewish eyes narrowed and her nostrils flared like a rhino about to charge, but she was stopped in her tracks. Charlie leaned down from his top bunk, whispered something to her in Chinese, smiled, then rolled over, snuggled down and went back to sleep. Dragon lady froze, blushed, and then turned and left the compartment as meek as a lamb. Unheard of. We woke Charlie and demanded to know the secret formula.

'Easy,' he said. 'I told her that I was going to let go of the blankets and she could pull them off. But she should first know that underneath it, I had the most enormous capitalist erection.'

The Foreign Office language training is nothing if not thorough.

AEROPLANES

Orson Welles was right when he declared, 'There are only two emotions in a plane: boredom and terror.'

I have vowed that, after we retire, I shall not set foot in

an airport again unless absolutely necessary. I am sick of rubber eggs and coffee that tastes of boiled underwear; sick of petulant aircrews and uncomfortable seats: sick of being irradiated like a Marks & Spencer's prawn.

Air travel is to be avoided if at all possible. Charlie swears he has seen an air stewardess hit the roof, although this was due to turbulence rather than his refusal to put his seat back into the upright position. But if you travel extensively, you have to accept that there will be times when you have no choice but to travel at night, in fog or through thunderstorms. And sometimes there is no way to avoid certain airlines: when the in-flight meal is a slice of spam and the air stewardess has not shaved that morning, I always make a point of having a little chat with my Maker in case I have to drop in unexpectedly.

Airlines do not always do much to promote peace of mind. The aptly pronounced CAAC, China's airline in the 1980s, was desperately trying to turn itself into a modern international airline. I remember when they first introduced a safety video instead of the stewardesses pointing out the safety procedures. It was entitled 'In-flight Annunciation', which was slightly alarming for all of us lapsed Catholics on board.

On one flight across China the woman across the aisle pulled open the magazine pocket on the back of the seat in front of her and chundered heartily into it resulting in a rhythmic dripping throughout the rest of the flight. On another, in the heat of a Chinese summer, they kept us on board on the tarmac for several hours without air conditioning. The man in front had just killed his favourite chicken before boarding, intending that it should still be fresh for his family on arrival. The chicken was rapidly getting higher and higher while we, unfortunately, stayed resolutely on the ground. By the time we finally took off, it was a half-baked, festering health hazard and could probably have walked the distance on its own.

Our friend Piers Litherland, who worked for the merchant bank Jardine's in China, had a particularly horrible experience on a flight from Tibet. I cannot do justice to the whole harrowing tale, but after losing his luggage, getting locked up overnight in a Tibetan monastery and being bitten by a rabid dog, he had to leave Tibet in a hurry to get the essential rabies injections before he started to froth at the mouth. Half-way through his mercy flight back to Chengdu he realized that something was very wrong with the aeroplane. It was. The wing-flaps were refusing to move, which meant that the plane could not slow down. The pilot radioed ahead to warn the emergency services, as the plane descended in swoops and landed at full speed. The tyres burst on impact, as the plane swerved, skewed and screeched its way full pelt down the runway. The passengers in the brace position clutched the back of their heads in terror as the overhead lockers burst open and deposited their contents on the passengers underneath.

Oxygen masks dangled and flopped around their heads as the cabin filled with smoke and the stink of metal grinding on tarmac. As the plane finally juddered to a halt two inches from the perimeter fence, Piers managed to look out of the window to see the arrival of the Chengdu Emergency Services. Slopping along the grass verge, making his way as fast as he could on a very old bicycle, was a man with his trouser legs rolled up wearing a scruffy pair of bedroom slippers. He had with him a solitary bucket of water hanging from his handlebars.

No matter how awful flying on your own is, flying *en famille* is a thousand times worse, especially if the children are in the projectile vomiting, screaming, snot-smearing, smelly stage, which usually lasts until they are about seventeen.

I once followed a trail of diarrhoea up the aisle of the plane at the beginning of a ten-hour flight from New Zealand to Hong Kong, only to find that it led right to my seat, where my fourteen-month-old son, beaming with joy, was bobbing up and down, oblivious to the liquid silage squirting out of both sides of his nappy. I have a special affection for Air New Zealand, who could not have been sweeter about my ruining their aeroplane. Air New Zealand is the airline, incidentally, where an air stewardess, over-come by desire or medication, stripped off and tried to seduce a male passenger. Weeks later, as an Air New Zealand plane was starting its descent into Auckland, the

captain requested everyone to return to their seats, fasten their seat-belts and return the air hostess to the upright position. Imagine BA saying that.

Some people actually dope their children up before a long flight. The only trouble with the drug concerned was that it sometimes backfired and had the opposite effect, leaving you with a pigmy-sized fizz-bomb to deal with all night.

Because of Charlie's annoying habit of always saying that tasks were 'simple' when they obviously were not, I refused point-blank to take our two infants back from Hong Kong on my own unless Charlie 'I-don't-know-why-you're-making-such-a-fuss' did it first. And, surprisingly enough, he did. I was hugely impressed. What a 'new man' I had married. Weeks later back in Hong Kong, I was bewildered by numerous strange women who kept coming up and greeting my children like old friends. 'Who was that?' I asked Freddie, my daughter.

'Just one of the ladies who looked after us on the flight home. Daddy was asleep.'

Single women on aeroplanes, especially those travelling with children, have completely different travelling experiences from those of single men. Charlie always flirts like a train with the check-in assistant or pretends that he has an injured leg from a skiing accident and always gets upgraded. When I try it, I am told, rather sarcastically, to take a Nurofen. I believe that there is a special place in hell for people who obtain upgrades by deceitful means. There, for eternity, they will be strapped into a row of seats next to someone grossly obese, who has not washed, who talks incessantly and suffers from irritable bowels.

This discrepancy in treatment between the sexes gave rise to what I like to think of as a rare display of blatant rudeness on my part. I was travelling back from Hong Kong on my own, revelling in my child-free status, but being continually bugged by the fluttering, giggling flirtations going on between the stewardess and the surrounding businessmen. I come from a family of four large-bottomed, no-nonsense women, and simpering always makes me growl.

Nine hours into the flight our breakfast arrived. We were all groggy and grumpy as we tucked into rubber eggs and propped our magazines up in front of us, so that we could avoid chatting. It was at that moment that the sweet little stewardess leant over the businessman on my left, picked up my magazine, shut it and slid it behind my back. 'In India, we have a saying,' she fluttered, wrinkling her little nose at the businessman, 'that if you read at meal times, you offend both the God of Food and the God of Literature.'

I felt that growl rising up from somewhere deep in my being.

Retrieving the magazine and putting it back on my table, I replied, 'In England we have a saying that if you read at breakfast, it means "fuck off".' It felt great.

Now after so many years of family flying, a strange sort of numbness descends every time I enter an airport and I find myself going through the motions on autopilot. At Heathrow the other day I was half-way through my Pret a Manger sandwich before I realized that I had left my shoes behind at the security X-ray machine and had been shuffling around Duty Free in my socks.

Still, next time you are cursing yourself or agreeing to fly Aeroflotsam or Jetsam, as the turbulence forces your bladder higher than your tonsils and the man next to you considers deodorant an expense too far, remember:

It could have been worse: you could have stayed at home.

4
Entertaining Abroad

*The abominable sin of sodomy is tolerated here, and all
over China, and so is buggery, which they use both with
beasts and fowls, in so much that Europeans do not care
to eat duck.*

(Alexander Hamilton, 1727)

*How to swallow revolting things without losing your dignity
or supper*

EYE OF NEWT AND LEG OF FROG

We have all heard the stories: the cook who made mayon-
naise by spraying the olive oil into the bowl from his
mouth; or the chef, whose secret swigs at the sherry

decanter were replaced by fluid of his own making, the Ambassador's wife who then served it to her bridge four and the visiting Minister, who admired its salty impertinence.

It takes someone who has been forcibly amputated from the joys of Waitrose to appreciate these tales. The difficulties of gathering people of every conceivable nationality, size, shape and religion around a dining table and being able to feed them despite all their dietary fads, restrictions and allergies are almost insurmountable, especially when all you could buy in the market that week were cabbage and chicken's feet. Add to that weevils in your self-raising flour and your home-help retiring to bed after her internal organs have been shrivelled by a voodoo enchantment, and you have the beginnings of an overseas dinner party. As for dietary restrictions, I once had to cook a dinner party for a group who consisted of a Jewish couple, one of whom was diabetic, two vegans, one person suffering from coeliac disease and one who was allergic to dairy products. Oh, and one nut allergy. As far as I can remember, I gave them each a lightly grilled button mushroom and a stick of celery – all halal, just in case I missed something.

When you arrive in a new place, just trying to work out which things in the local market are fit for human consumption can take a while. How to make them edible can take another few weeks. I always try things out on Charlie first: if it makes him nauseous or dizzy, I save it for dinner with the French. It's somehow inevitable that, on the night of your first dinner party in a new posting, the power fails, the gas runs out and your hired-in help tells you it is good luck to spit in the soup (but not to worry, as he has already done the honours).

My first shopping outing in Peking involved a trip to the only vaguely Westernized outlet in town, the infamous Friendship Store, a huge emporium selling everything from heavy Chinese lacquer ware to cabbage. In fact often all it sold was heavy Chinese lacquer ware and cabbage. In the food hall, which was filthy, deliveries would arrive and sell out within minutes. So the rule was, if you saw it, grab it. Grab all of it, as you might not see it again for a year.

Running down the centre of the hall was a bank of open freezers filled with gently defrosting bags of innards. Each section had its own handwritten card, smeared with bloody fingerprints like a psychopath's Christmas list. First there was 'Pig Mince', then 'Cow mince', then 'Stomachs', then 'Ears'. Things were already moving out of my range of experience. My eyes nearly popped out of my head as I moved on to the next freezer, where the sign read 'Cocks'. I was just beginning to plan some exotic, if somewhat vulgar menus, when I noticed that the next sign, rather

disappointingly, said 'Hens'.

Food supplies were so dire in the Friendship Store that a New Zealand friend, Lucy Worker, received a book from her mother back at home entitled *100 Things to Do with Dried Egg* (or 'Dried Igg', as they would say in Auckland). There was even a recipe going round at the time for making your own cream. It involved margarine and a lot of wrist work. I ended up with a strange, snot-like slime, which refused to go down the plughole when I tried to chuck it away.

In fact, it was nearly always possible to get hold of eggs, but other staples were either hard to come by or a bit odd. The sugar was definitely strange. One attempt at meringues resulted in liquid glucose oozing out of the oven and running all over the kitchen floor. I scrubbed that floor many times, but to no avail. Thereafter, the moment the lights went out, a billion small cockroaches would appear to lick off the sugary veneer. Any visitor needing a glass of water at night was advised to steer clear of the kitchen, because after dark the floor became a seething crunchy mass of wriggling, articulated outer skeleton.

I always find it rather sweet that the Americans call

them Chinese cockroaches and the Chinese call them American cockroaches. I just call them repulsive bastards and have done with it. For a while, after dinner parties, I would clear away all the food and dishes before we went to bed, but leave the tablecloth on. In the morning it always seemed to have poppy seeds scattered all over it. I later found out that the poppy seeds were in fact cockroach eggs, which changed my slovenly habits overnight.

A friend in the flat downstairs had a novel approach. He only ever attempted insecticide using his feet and a leap of at least a metre no matter where the victim was crawling. His wife, Kay, eventually banned him from karate-kicking the walls, because the shoe marks and squished remains detracted even from a Communist's idea of superior décor.

Trying to cater with restricted ingredients can lead to desperate measures. A certain South American Ambassador in Saudi Arabia a few years ago was stopped in his car at the border and asked about his dog.

'It is a Mexican hairless Chihuahua,' he replied, stroking its little pink head. They were allowed through and the Chihuahua thrived happily until full grown, whereupon one day he mysteriously disappeared and the smell of frying bacon spread across the land, happily unrecognizable to the local population.

In Libya, in a moment of desperation, I fed spaghetti Tripolinese made with camel to two of Barney's friends out for the holidays. Having wolfed down one bowl quite happily thinking it was beef, they refused seconds when I let slip that they were digesting camel. This strange reluctance from the boys of course led to an exploration of camel cuisine. We enjoyed camelloni, meat loaf with a hump, Bactrian Bourguignonne; I was just warming to the theme, when Charlie called a halt and begged for a steak. (I had not even got to my Ship of the Dessert.)

Camel is rather tame compared to the dinner served by one of the more adventurous Foreign Office types to have passed through our lives. One of his responsibilities in Hong Kong was to keep an eye on the language students. He had invited a group of them over to his flat for dinner, and as they were studying Chinese he wanted to give them something really authentic. He tripped off to the local market in his lunch-hour, bought everything he needed and, once back in the office, stuffed it all into the bottom drawer of his desk. He then left for a meeting. While he was away a colleague went into his drawer where she stumbled on the supper ingredients, still live, writhing and hissing

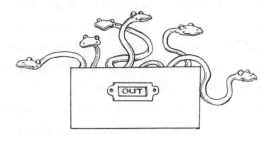

and looking for an escape route from their dark dungeon. The Head of Mission took a Dim View of live snakes being brought into his bailiwick. He wrote a report to London: 'I have warned this man about his eccentricities. I am all for eccentrics, but not in the British Trade Commission. Although I am assured that the snakes had had their venom removed, I am not so sure. I have instructed him not to bring live animals into the Commission again.'

Years later our adventurous friend gave me a small bottle containing what looked like frogsnot. 'That,' he assured me, 'is the most powerful aphrodisiac known to man. It is brewed in Mongolia and treasured beyond yaks.' To our eternal, miserable, middle-class shame Charlie and I never tried it, and now I am too shy and much too old to ask for some more.

THE DINNER DEATH EXPERIENCE

My first-ever diplomatic dinner party was a disaster. I had discovered through a series of embarrassing misunderstandings that foreigners are in fact a lot more formal than Brits, so I had gone all out to do things properly. I had invited a number of young diplomats from other embassies in Peking, including a charming Spaniard married to a bubbly Iranian called Nasi, whose English was a roller-coaster ride with no handrails or safety-belts. You never knew where your conversations with Nasi were headed or where you would end up, but it was always a surprise, usually a delight and sometimes (my favourite) jaw-droppingly embarrassing. Her Iranian accent, with its rolling Rs and her Zsa Zsa Gabor 'darlinks', was irresistible.

For the starter I had managed to find some quail's eggs in a market on the other side of the Forbidden City – definitely a first. I decided on a jelly of beef consommé with cream cheese on the bottom and a quail egg on the top (I know . . . but it was very trendy at the time).

Unfortunately, the consommé did not set. In desperation I shoved all the ramekins in the freezer. By the time we sat down to dinner they had frozen rock solid and risen out of their little china dishes like miniature volcanoes, out of the top of which popped pebble-hard, jet-black quail's eggs, for all the world like ebony nipples. The guests chipped, carved, tried crampons and dynamite, but to no avail.

The next course was worse. The meat was so chewy that people were actually giving up and spitting it back out again. Just when I thought things could not get any worse, Nasi decided to distract everyone with a little discourse on romance. Our embassy was home to a wonderful young First Secretary called Claire Stubbs, whose love life was Nasi's main preoccupation: her sole aim on waking was to get Claire hitched to a man.

During a horrible lull, while the wife of the Bulgarian

Press Attaché was gagging over a piece of beef which had only gone half-way down and was now bungee-jumping up her throat again, Nasi returned to her theme; her sexy Iranian accent reverberating around my dining-room at full throttle.

'What Claire Stubbs needs,' she declared in a voice you could have heard in North Korea, 'what Claire Stubbs needs is a cunt.'

Everything stopped. Charlie had the perplexed look on his face of a man trying to find the words to reassure Nasi that he thought Claire was fully equipped in that department without appearing too knowledgeable on the matter. The foreign guests who weren't familiar with the word were looking with raised eyebrows at those who obviously were. They, in turn, were looking at Charlie for guidance out of this sticky diplomatic quagmire. After what seemed like a month of electric silence, Nasi continued:

'A cunt, or a duke, or an earl. Someone with a *tiiitle*, darlink.'

There was the deafening sound of eyebrows being lowered, and the great whoosh of expelled relief nearly snuffed out my candles. Claire is still my friend and has moved on to greater things, but no matter how grown up and important she is every time I see her, I have to stop myself thinking, 'What Claire Stubbs needs . . .'

I wish that had been my last dinner-party disaster, but unfortunately they seem to just keep on happening. In

HOW TO EAT A MANGO

1.
Cut the mango
around its middle.

2.
Take hold of each
half and twist sharply
in different directions.

3.
Pull apart
and eat the half
without the stone.

4.
Using the empty
skin as a grip take
hold of the stone &
twist it out of the
remaining half.

5.
Eat the remaining
half straight away
or drop into a fancy
glass and fill with
fresh fruit and
cream.

Libya, the plaster from my right index finger went missing in action somewhere in the depths of the saffron chicken with the French Ambassador due in half an hour. I went through the entire dish with a pair of tweezers, and found it with only ten minutes to spare. I do realize that in owning up to this I risk no one in their right minds ever again accepting a dinner invitation at my house, but in future, if I cut myself slicing onions, I shall stick the plaster on with superglue and put on a pair of those immigration-officer rubber gloves which go all the way up to your armpits. If I lose one of those in your saffron chicken it will be a lot easier to find than a tiny plaster.

Wherever you move to abroad, you have to improvise for the things that you cannot find in the local market. Beware of the familiar. One lemon in Cyprus equals three from Tesco. Meat behaves differently in every country I have ever been to. Eggs can taste of fish. Water has sometimes to be so sterilized that it is like cooking with swimming-pool water. On the other hand when fresh mangoes arrived in the Friendship Store, life would stop for a while. Potatoes in Cyprus are better than I have had anywhere else in the world, and the vegetables in Libya taste of sunshine, even if it is hard to get the sand off.

One warning though: the spices in the Middle East are almost radioactive compared to the timid stuff you get in the West. Cumin in particular should be locked up tightly in a screwtop jar, because the flavour is so strong it creeps through every ingredient in your cupboard. I once served cumin-flavoured treacle tart with pine nuts. I pretended it was a new Heston Blumenthal recipe – very chic and quite the new thing. Actually it was revolting.

Despite all the hassle of entertaining abroad, often it is the location which makes the occasion memorable. We have enjoyed picnics among the deserted Ming Tombs outside Peking with the temperature at minus 20 degrees. We have had barbecues cooked on an open fire under the stars on an empty beach in the Karpas and then drifted with the current in warm black water, finding our way back guided by the embers of the fire. We have eaten fresh, crusty *shwarma* sitting on a kerb in the mountains on the Israel–Lebanon border, being lectured by a Druze on the Palestinian problem.

A couple of our most memorable dinners have been with our Canadian friends, John and Martine Sloan. In those days restaurants in Peking were scarce and pretty uninspiring. We wanted to find a novel location to give John a special dinner on his birthday, but one that was away from the teeming masses of people – a difficult task in one of the planet's most populous spots. In the end we broke out on to the roof of our apartment block, one of the tallest buildings in Peking, and served up dinner looking out over the lights of the Forbidden City. Candles, Edith Piaf on the stereo, and peace. After dinner John pulled the tiny Martine on his lap. He leant back smoking his cigar

HOW
TO MAKE
LEBANESE
LEMONADE

1.

Measure out equal quantities of
freshly squeezed lemon juice and sugar.

2.

Place in a saucepan
with a sprig of sweet
geranium.

3.

Bring to the boil,
stirring until the sugar
melts.

4.

— remove —
geranium
leaves

←water

lemonade →

— add —
water

When cool, bottle and keep in the fridge.
If you want ·PINK LEMONADE· add a spoonful
of POMEGRANATE molasses.

and closed his eyes. 'After all these years,' he said to her, 'I still love the way you stroke my face.'

'But, John, I am not stroking your face.'

There was a three-inch cockroach crawling up his right cheek.

Dining out on the Great Wall of China completely alone – watching its long scaly back winding around us, changing colour as the buttery sun melted beneath the horizon – must rank as one of our most memorable experiences of beauty. The section of the wall we had chosen was then unrestored: ancient, huge and silent. Here you could walk or scramble for hours, skimming along the very tops of the mountains, at one point curling along the top of an enormous precipice, at another winding softly around the contours of a hidden valley filled with almond trees. The mountains in China always appear sharper to me than others, whittled by the sand-laden winds from the Gobi desert into arthritic-fingered peaks, the rocks sculpted down to their bones, pricking a sky of bleached skin.

It was here we said goodbye to John Sloan, who went next morning direct from the Great Wall to the airport and back to Canada. Twelve of us packed a feast on our backs and through the hot evening haze trudged up and up through the scrubby forest to the most beautiful part of the wall we knew. We were completely alone – so rare in China. The only sound was the distant call of some peasant to his ox. It was utterly tranquil. Between crumbling Ming towers we drank wine and watched the purple mists collect in the valley hollows. All night I lay awake listening to the clicking of the insects and the occasional screech from an owl or its prey, until the dawn wind picked up, blowing through the windows of the watchtowers, following ancient stones down to the sea.

DEATH FOR QUEEN AND COUNTRY

Never underestimate the usefulness of official entertaining. When ice needs to be broken, when friendships need to be forged and contacts consolidated, what better tool to use than food and drink? On the other hand, when revenge needs to be exacted or punishment meted out there is no better method of showing displeasure and disapproval than the starchy diplomatic dinner party.

For centuries the official dinner has been used as an extension of the battlefield. When the Libyan Mohammed Ali needed to rid himself of the troublesome Egyptian Mamelukes in 1807, he invited them all over for a barbecue, wined and dined them handsomely, and then had them all kebabed on the way out. Over four hundred of them were skewered in one sitting. Nowadays, of course, government cutbacks would probably require all the dispatching to be undertaken *before* dinner, thereby saving

HMG the restaurant bill, but it would be a slightly less elegant manoeuvre.

Lord McCarthy, who led the first trade mission to China, complained that when negotiating with the Chinese, food and drink were withheld as a tool to force the British to concede certain points. I rather got the impression that they were doing the same during the Hong Kong handover talks 200 years later. Mind you, the British negotiating team got their revenge by exploiting the Chinese weakness for seasickness. There is nothing as upsetting for a non-seafaring nation as a dinner on one of Hong Kong's outlying islands preceded by a long bucketing junk trip. Anyone who has ever been in a Chinese junk will

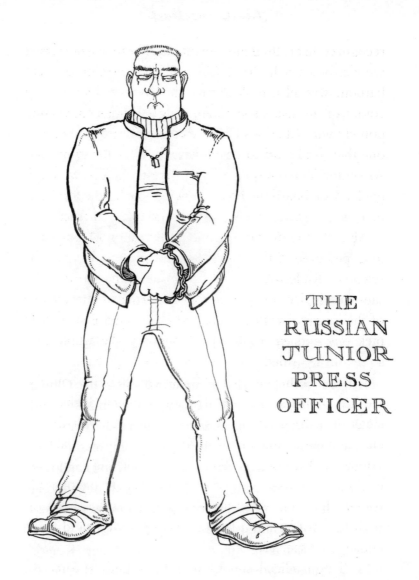

THE
RUSSIAN
JUNIOR
PRESS
OFFICER

recognize that rolling movement peculiar to flat-bottomed wooden boats in the South China Sea. Three minutes out of harbour was all it took to turn the average diplomat the colour of the sea. I spent agonizing evenings conversing politely with Charlie's Chinese counterparts, until one by one they broke off to heave heartily over the gunwales. After dinner in some jolly island fish restaurant we would all get back on board the boat, knowing that all the food that had just been eaten was about to return to the surface.

Actually the history of food as a weapon of war has a long pedigree. Otto von Bismarck once challenged the scientist, Rudolf Vorchow, to a duel. The latter chose sausages in place of swords or pistols. He had infected one of the sausages with cholera and challenged Bismarck to pick one and eat it. Bismarck thought the whole idea so revolting he fled. No doubt he feared the wurst.

Charlie has never flinched in the service of his country. He has chomped his way through jellyfish, ducks' feet, slugs, deep-fried scorpions, donkey burger, assorted testicles, unmentionable innards, turtles, frog-snot, swallows' vomit, snake, dog, camel's hump, yak's eye and my cooking. He was even offered bear's paw on one trip round China and when he drew the line at this, his hosts tried to insist he ate it because next year it would be an endangered species.

Although official entertainment is usually a force for good, it can also have an evil hidden agenda. It is the perfect stage for those subtle nuances of insult or favour that Europeans enjoy so much, a multi-layered menued metaphor for each guest to employ as he or she wishes, course by course.

I, of course, am the Rambo of the dinner-party set. Where others use the delicate epée of etiquette, I prefer the no-nonsense cluster-bomb of the social gaffe. I can make grown men cry just by unfolding my napkin. From upsetting Islamic dinner companions by miming keep fit – they thought that I was mocking their method of praying – to shouting 'Good luck with your wife coming' to an Egyptian waiter, whose wife I knew to be having visa problems getting into Libya, if there is a hole to fall into, I will jump in all on my own. At a Chinese banquet I spun the Lazy Susan in the centre of the table with such enthusiasm that the protruding serving spoons knocked over all the wine glasses, one by one, sending China's No. 1 Great Wall claret cascading over everyone's deep-fried noodles with pig's intestines, radically changing the recipe to soup. And I was completely sober.

I am not a great drinker. Most Brits can knock back a few without falling over, but a large glass of Lucozade has me slurring my words and telling everyone that I love them. So it was with a certain amount of incredulity that I found myself coerced into a drinking competition with a particularly unpleasant Chinese official. A truly nasty man, he was rumoured to have tortured American prisoners in Korea and covered himself in gory glory during the Cultural Revolution. He had one of those bland, moon faces that only give away the evil they contain when they smile. His talent obviously lay in finding people's weaknesses and he zoned in on me to match him toast for toast. I wouldn't normally have risen to the challenge, but he was so unpleasant that I didn't want to let him win. (That and Charlie giving me his 'Well, I won't hold the sick bowl' face.)

The utterly revolting spirit we had to down was called Maotai. It is so strong that it can burn at room temperature. It must have a slow absorption rate because, strangely, I kept going for a surprisingly long time. After what seemed to be at least six bottles' worth he called a truce. We said our goodbyes and with my head held high I walked in a beautiful straight line to the car. I had not disgraced myself in any way: I could still speak in coherent sentences, I had not told strangers that I wanted to have their babies and I had not vomited into anyone's handbag.

Then it hit me. As we drove away, the Maotai slammed into my central nervous system like a sledgehammer. Charlie, laughing his horrible head off, had to grog-march me into the lift and carry me to bed, where I spent the next two days groaning and belching up foul-tasting reminders of the evil evening. Still I like to think that I did my country proud, even if it did nearly cost me the use of my legs.

At least I did not end up like one famous female correspondent I met on my first night out in Hong Kong. It was rather an exciting dinner with lots of journalists, who swapped war stories like recipes and drank far more than they ate. During a rather racy story about a gun and a bloodstain on the carpet of the Foreign Correspondents' Club, I noticed that the famous female correspondent opposite me was sliding very slowly and elegantly down her chair and under the table, still clutching her tumbler full of whisky in one hand and a cigarette in the other. There she stayed for the rest of the evening, occasionally reaching up for a light or a refill, and shouting the odd rude remark from somewhere down by my left foot.

The incident of the evil drinking competition did result in a golden nugget of good advice from a colleague. Should you ever find yourself having to survive awful toasts at official dinners, when to refuse that nation's national drink of Maotai, schnapps, fermented goat urine would cause great offence, here it is.

At the end of dinner before the toasts start, ensure that you have two glasses in front of you, one with an inch or so of water and one with Coke. When the toasting begins, clink your glass, look your host in the eye, throw your head back and fill your mouth with whatever paint-stripper they have given you, *but do not swallow*. Just pretend to do so. Roll your eyes, smile, squeak as if it is simply marvellous and then after a decent pause pick up

the soft drink glass as though for a sip and discreetly spit the foul brew into the matching colour, i.e. Maotai into the water, filthy Armenian brandy into the Coke.

You will maintain your dignity while everyone else is losing theirs.

THE NATIONAL DAY NIGHTMARE

Whoever invented National Days should be shot. On second thoughts, they should have spring rolls stuffed up their nose, be tied to a flagpole in a freezing garden and forced to listen to the Greek National Anthem.

Most National Day celebrations are more boring than you can possibly imagine. At least the Queen's Birthday Party has a little pzazz, especially if there is a military band involved, preferably with its ceremonial goat. In Cyprus the regimental goat was courtmartialled for mounting the band-master during the Last Post. That sort of thing always livens up proceedings.

The Dutch embassy once inflicted a performance of

their national synchronized-swimming team on everyone at their National Day. Hour after hour of watching sturdy, goose-pimpled and relentlessly smiling girls sploshing about in the deep end and waving their legs in the air. Hideous.

The Cypriots have a good old-fashioned military parade on their day. The trouble is that, as with all things Cypriot, they never know when to call it a day. Every military, police, fire, social-worker unit on the island has its march past. I loved the SAS equivalent with their skis – there is one small mountain on Cyprus which occasionally has snow – and the SBS equivalent whose soldiers had to march in full underwater kit, including snorkel, mask and flippers.

The Russians have a fun evening. All the women dress up like Joan Collins out of *Dynasty* with big, big hairdos held rigidly in position with an entire ozone layer of hair-spray. The military attachés try to look relaxed in their badly fitting uniforms or suits, but their necks are wider than their heads and their arms don't bend. In the days of the Cold War in Peking, instead of a party, they used to invite the foreign community to play them at ice hockey on their embassy lake. Charlie convinced the Canadians, Swedes and Finns that his wicket-keeping skills were translatable into goalkeeping (or tending, as they call it, rather gently). It was a bit like watching your husband being beaten up in slow motion. He was pummelled, thwacked, flattened and winded, often all at the same time and usually by the Russian Ambassador's driver, who was built like a steel mill.

Chinese National Day is always worth attending because the food is so good, except for one year when their chefs didn't separate the sweet dishes from the savoury. Everyone piled their plates with spring rolls and noodles, dim sum and butterfly prawns, and poured what they thought to be sweet and sour sauce over everything. It turned out to be a sweet, sickly strawberry custard. The looks of desperation as greedy ambassadors ploughed through the sticky messes on their plates were heaven to behold. We lesser mortals managed to dump our plates behind pot plants, but the higher echelons were truly hoisted and had to suffer slowly, bite by gooey bite.

Official entertaining was beautifully summed up on a flyer I received from a Libyan chef touting for business. 'Catering and Undertaking', it read.

Quite.

5
Home-Help Hell

*Militants are like cleaning women, doing a thankless,
daily but necessary job.*

(François Truffaut)

Learning to love your cleaning lady more than life itself

HOME-HELP HELL

I am a complete amateur in the housekeeping department.
Chaos and mess is my natural habitat and I can instantly
get rid of dirt simply by removing my glasses.

A clean house is an empty mind; a car is a wheelie bin
with an engine and gardening is the opium of the middle
classes.

In other words, I am bone idle.

As a wishy-washy liberal, I find employing nice people to do my dirty work rather shameful, but laziness beats shame hand over fist every time, so I bite down hard on the bullet of my social conscience and get in help. Think of it as trickling down wealth and you will be amazed how easy it becomes.

The only nugget of advice I feel qualified to give is, wherever possible, employ locals rather than bring in reinforcements from home. Importing an English nanny to drill young Sebastian in perfect table manners may seem a good idea at the time, but employing a local is much more fun. They may cook fermented beancurd, give you intimate details of their period problems over breakfast, and have some bizarre ideas about God, which they would love to share with you, but they also know their way around, and have a network of friends already in place. They can also teach your children to swear fruitily in the local slang. Altogether more useful than learning how to greet a bishop.

I can tell you about nannies, cleaning ladies, guards and gardeners, all of whom I have had experience. I know little about cooks, because that is one part of the domestic hard core that I quite enjoy doing myself, or about drivers, as I have never had one. All the others I have loved and learnt from. They have emptied the house of dirt and filled it with laughter and scandalous stories. What more could a girl want?

NANNIES

Our first posting 'with children' was Hong Kong. Freddie was three years old and Barnaby was born at the Matilda hospital two months after we arrived. To give some continuity we decided to bring out our existing nanny from London. We were ensconced in the Hong Kong Hotel, while looking for a flat, when she arrived at Kai Tak airport. It was her first time living abroad and she was ready to make the most of it. Penny was a pocket Venus. A fire-cracker of a girl. Of Portuguese extraction, she was fiery, funny and had a head-tossing temper, mixed with a sunny smile and a glorious unpredictability.

Her arrival at the hotel caused quite a stir. She sashayed across the lobby wearing nothing but high heels, a very short skirt and a black lacy bra. Charlie, who had gone to fetch her, walked behind her, waving his arms at me and mouthing 'DO SOMETHING'. I felt a 'talk' coming on. I explained to Penny that although Hong Kong was very hot, it was also very conservative and that maybe her outfit was a little too much for the good *taitais* of Kowloon: abroad was, after all, a 'foreign country and they do things differently there'. Word about Penny's fashion statement spread rapidly around the hotel like beginning-of-term lice at a Montessori. The next morning at breakfast, at least four teenage girls came down wearing tiny

mini-skirts, black lacy bras and a smirk, while their fathers sat steaming with fury, giving us the evil eye.

A year later the Hong Kong party scene took Penny off with an Australian boyfriend and the process of interviewing for a replacement began. I was battle-hardened by this time and had listed all the things I required in a child-minder. I was ready to interrogate each applicant ruthlessly.

The first interviewee arrived, a round, smiling woman in her late thirties from the Philippines. Before I had time to ask her any of my prepared questions, she said: 'My name is Bing. I realize that you won't want to employ me, because I have one leg shorter than the other and I limp.'

She stayed with us for nine years.

Bing's hobby was voodoo witchcraft. I say 'hobby', but it was more a lifestyle. Her world was inhabited by ghouls and hobgoblins. Ghosts of dead children sat on her shoulder whispering winning lottery numbers in her ears and wild spirits scratched at her window at night. Sometimes in the morning she would show me bruises which she had sustained defending her honour from sex-crazed incubi in the dark hours. Weird concoctions were brewed in the kitchen to keep these ne'er-do-wells at bay, and crazy

Tagalog incantations were muttered over pans of bubbling green soup while the children ate their supper.

After our return to London the other children in the street thought that she was the coolest nanny on the block, although I did get a few complaints from their parents, when her tales of baby-eating boggarts and evil floating monks got a little too graphic.

The upside of Bing was that she made me see London with new eyes. On first looking out of our kitchen window at the grey March skies, she asked, round-eyed, if this was the rainy season. She was amazed at the flowers on the horse-chestnut trees and collected conkers like a prep-school boy. Freddie and Barney teased her mercilessly, but loved her to pieces. They fell asleep singing Filipino protest songs instead of lullabies.

The downside was that my son grew up with a strong Filipino accent and could chant quasi-religious incantations before he could talk. We once crept up on him sitting up in bed, crooning, 'Loord, leestin to myee cryeein.' My beautiful blonde daughter spurned the trendy dungarees I bought her in favour of pink, frothy, fire-hazard frocks, which Bing had found in the Sunday markets. For six months I had to walk around with a souped-up, Barbie-pink, glittery princess on my arm. It was like having a miniature drag-queen as a pet.

The main problem with Bing, and one we never quite managed to cure her of, was her obsession with her insides, particularly her woman's bits. After years of living abroad I have discovered that it is only British women who keep their internal affairs private. Everyone else discusses them in graphic, no-holds- or holes-barred detail.

My husband is a simple man. He believes that any conversation should start after breakfast and should never include the workings of the female reproductive system. This was a cultural divide to which Bing remained forever oblivious.

'Oh, serr,' she would groan, as he communed with his Weetabix, 'today I am feeling very *bloated*.'

This would be followed up with intimate details of ebbing and flowing, high and low tides, until Charlie fled, white-faced, to finish his breakfast locked in the bathroom. In the end I had to tell her that my husband came from a strange family where it had been tradition never to speak until one had digested breakfast and thanked the good Lord. She could relate to this, but she still only had to say 'Oh, serr' at any time and he would bolt for the door. To this day if any member of the family has designs on the last roast potato and Charlie is a contender, they only have to breath the word 'bloated' in his ear and he loses his appetite.

When we were about to leave London on another posting and had to send the children to boarding school, Bing surprised us by announcing that she had married a much younger man on her last trip to the Philippines. He had stayed there looking after all the houses she had accumulated while working for us. She left us to go to work for Nicky Clarke, the hairdresser. We missed her butter tarts, her bossiness and her winning lottery numbers, but I like to think of her casting voodoo spells all over St John's Wood.

CLEANING LADIES

In the broad spectrum of the family's relations with cleaning ladies we go from the diabolical to the sublime. The sublime being Andrea, who came to save us in Cyprus. Before her arrival we had a little trouble with our cleaning ladies. There were family problems, husband problems, visa problems and, of course, 'bloating' problems. We thought that we were eventually in calm waters when we settled on

HOW TO CLEAN DUSTY SILK FLOWERS

1.

Fill a large plastic bag with 2-3 inches of table salt.

2.

Place flowers head down in the bag.

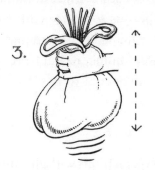

3.

Shake vigorously.

4.

Remove flowers.

The dust and dirt clings to the salt. You are left with a brand new, refreshed bunch of flowers and a bag of disgustingly dirty salt.

a very energetic and jolly woman, who was great at cleaning and danced rather seductively as she vacuumed.

'How do you keep in such great shape?' I asked one day.

She raised her arms above her head, jerked her hips in a definite *ba-boom* motion and screamed with laughter: 'Sex, lots of sex.'

Alarm bells rang. I have nothing against nympho-maniacs, but it would probably not be good for Anglo-Cypriot relations to have a senior diplomat's house used as a brothel, even if the décor suggested it already was one. I suspect there is something in Diplomatic Service Procedure against using taxpayers' money for promoting that type of thing. I was still debating how to deal with the matter, when a week later I came down the stairs to find a completely strange lady vacuuming my carpet. 'Hello,' I said. 'Where's Sally?'

'She cannot come today.'

'Is she in bed?'

'No. She in prison.'

'Oh my God! What for?' I asked, scared stiff that Nicosia Police Department's finest were about to break down the door, charge me with keeping a brothel and haul me off to join her.

'She selling babies.'

I was rather fond of babies, so Sally and her friends had to go, and the sublime Andrea walked into my life and my house. She said I was the messiest person she had ever met and ruled us with a rod of iron for the next three years. She never mentioned being bloated, but I could not cure her of the habit of saying she was going to change the 'shits' or teach her to pronounce 'finish' properly. It seems that Filipinas always pronounce an 'f' as a 'p' and a 'sh' as an 's'. Every time I asked her how work was going she would yell 'PENIS'. At the top of her voice. When the terrorists blew up London she came with tears in her eyes to tell me that there were 'bums' going off all over England. I loved her to pieces.

Just occasionally you get no choice in whom you

employ. My first cleaning lady was our old Ayi in Peking. The Chinese Diplomatic Service Bureau, who ran these things, just allotted you the cleaning lady at the top of the list. We were lucky enough to hit pay-dirt. She must have been in her late sixties and was as tiny and fine-boned as the rice sparrows, which the Chinese so love to eat whole. She was convinced that we were not eating properly, which was a bit rich as she was the size of one of my legs. She used to bring us bags of home-made dumplings, and if we hadn't eaten them by the time of her next visit, she would wag her fingers at me and squeeze my waist. Clearly it was a matter of prestige to have a fat employer, a certain avoirdupois being connected in the old Chinese mind with prosperity and a healthy diet.

Poor Ayi was required to hand back most of the wages we paid her to the Diplomatic Service Bureau. They were a nasty bunch, who controlled everything to do with foreigners, and their office was seven floors down underneath our kitchen window. She never told me how much it was that they took, but I suspect that a hefty whack went into their greasy pockets.

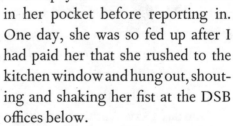

We later arranged a secret pay rise for her which she hid in her pocket before reporting in. One day, she was so fed up after I had paid her that she rushed to the kitchen window and hung out, shouting and shaking her fist at the DSB offices below.

'No, no, Ayi,' I said, dragging her back in. 'In England we do it like this.'

I stuck out my tongue and waved two fingers at them in a good old-fashioned Agincourt V sign.

From then on, every payday, this tiny, bird-like woman would hang out of my kitchen window and give the DSB two fingers for all her worth.

GUARDS

We have been lucky enough in our postings never to have needed guards until we got to Libya. I exclude Afghanistan, because I was not allowed to go. But in Tripoli two of the most delightful gentlemen you could ever wish to meet came into our lives, Anthony and Moses. They were both from Ghana, with gentle African good manners, generous laughs and pride in their work.

They had horribly long shifts, which at times must have been dull beyond words, but complaining was not in their natures. Anthony devoured books and would often recommend what he had been reading to me. In return I would hand over all my old thrillers, weeding out any I thought were too rude, because both Anthony and Moses were devout Christians.

One day I saw Anthony reading a large serious-looking tome. I asked what it was.

'Niall Ferguson's *Empire*, madam.' I made a mental note to improve the standard of paperbacks I was handing over and prayed that he would not expect me to read it too.

The embassy's security officer at this time was an ex-Royal Marine. Six foot three, with a very fierce moustache,

The worst case of squits I ever had was in Kabul in '92.....

lost control.....

nasty business.....

THE POLITICAL OFFICER

Basil would climb over the walls of the embassy houses at three o'clock in the morning to check whether the guards were awake. If he caught them asleep on the job, this was a serious matter: three strikes and you were out, and employment was hard to come by in Libya. Unfortunately, one night he found Anthony asleep.

In the morning I asked Anthony why he had dozed off.

'You see, madam,' he said in his soft Ghanaian accent, 'Niall Ferguson was just a little bit boring.' If Mr Ferguson ever meets Anthony, I think that he owes him a drink.

One of the most joyous occasions I have ever attended was Moses' wedding to his long-term girlfriend, Princess. She managed to get into Libya with the supporters of the Ghana football team and stayed, so that after many years of waiting she could get married. The wedding was over four hours long. It was a riot of colour and enthusiastic singing. Everyone laughed, clapped and joined in the vows.

'Will you, Moses, take Princess as your lawfully wedded wife?'

'I will.'

'Yeah, brother!'

'Hallelujah!'

Everyone yelled. Hymns were sung over and over again, gloriously. The sight of Charlie dancing round the church in a conga will stay with me for ever. This is the man who asked for his thirtieth birthday present never to have to dance again; a man with the sense of rhythm of a mushroom; a man whose stiff upper lip is spread over the rest of his body. There he was shuffling around the church, Praise God-ing and even wiggling his bottom a little.

Apart from Anthony all the embassy guards had the most wonderful names. There was Moses, Ezekiel, Solomon, Samuel, Jude and Noah.

One night after a party at the embassy club where the guards were earning extra money as waiters, Charlie and I gave three of the Old Testament prophets a lift home. Trevor, the First Secretary (Commercial), had just left post and had given Ezekiel his dog. It was a rather nasty Libyan dog, which I knew had bitten all of the guards. I remember being surprised when Trevor told me that Ezekiel had offered to take the dog on. He had certainly been a victim.

'So, Ezekiel,' I asked him, 'how is Mr Trevor's dog?'

Silence from the back of the car. Then solemnly, 'Mr Trevor's dog is in a very, very happy place.'

'Ezekiel, does that mean that Mr Trevor's dog is in a pie?'

Another silence. Then a broad grin spread across Ezekiel's face: 'Maybe!'

GARDENERS

We have only once had a garden, let alone a gardener, and that was in Cyprus. I am convinced that gardeners are the most intractable of breeds. The garden is theirs and you have no right to make even a suggestion. For a start, you are a foreigner, so how could you understand what is appropriate in the local climate? Then you have clearly never had dirt under your fingernails having lived in cities all your life. And if that were not enough, you are a woman. Case closed. My advice is that life is too stressful abroad to open a campaign on the horticultural front as well. I tried and failed. Whatever I planted was either pulled up, or deliberately over- or under-watered. And even if your command of the local language is sufficient to accuse the gardener of sabotage, you will not win. Save your sanity and start your own private plot on a balcony or a roof terrace, if you are lucky enough to have one.

Our gardener in Cyprus was huge and dark with flashing eyes and a great bushy black beard. He was as strong as an ox and only really happy when chopping things down, which he did with manic zeal. I never found out what he did during the Cyprus troubles, but he was a wild mountain man with a penchant for sharp knives and his strimmer.

At some point someone in the embassy must have said to me that he looked just like Jesus and I mistakenly heard it that his name was actually Jesus. For some months I happily called out to Jesus. 'Coffee, Jesus?' He never answered, but would flash his black eyes and grunt.

One morning in my kitchen I felt a huge shadow filling

the empty space behind me. A strong knobbly finger tapped me on the shoulder and I turned to see him standing quite close, wild-haired, sweating and covered in bits of twig and grass. More John the Baptist than Jesus. He thumped his chest with his fist, and then pointed it at me, waggling it slowly from side to side.

'No Jesus,' he growled. 'Stelios.' He then walked out of my kitchen, taking the biscuits. He was a lovely man, but always a little bit frightening. I found out through a complicated series of mimes that his daughter was to represent Cyprus in judo at the Peking Olympics. Not a family you would want to fall out with, I think. His English never got any better, but then neither did my Greek. But he, Andrea the cleaner and I would take our coffee breaks out of the sun under the lemon tree, with Andrea translating and flirting with Stelios in a wholly outrageous fashion. He would bring baskets of fruit from his farm and we would spoil him in return with expensive biscuits.

Before we left Cyprus Stelios came to say goodbye and he prodded me in the chest with his great, gnarled finger: 'You,' he rumbled in his deep, thunderous voice, 'You. Cyprus. Fat.' Then rubbing his hands, 'Good.'

I took it as a compliment, but Andrea thought that it was hilarious, and my last few weeks before she too left were punctuated by her whispering in my ear, 'You. Cyprus. Fat.'

6
Children Abroad

There are only two lasting bequests we can hope to give our children. One is roots; the other, wings.

(Hodding Carter)

Grow your own nomad — the ups and downs of raising your young on the hoof

THE BAEDEKER CHILDCARE GUIDE

We have two children. Freddie knows what she wants and works like a Trojan to get it. Barnaby is more of an Andrew Marvell man: the kind who expects ripe apples to fall about his head. (Much to our annoyance, they often do.) They both rather charmingly believe in fairies; in particular the fairy who picks up wet towels and beer cans,

and his little fairy friend who fills and empties the dishwasher. Despite the fact that they treat their parents with eye-rolling disdain, I cannot think of any two people I would rather spend time with. When they are at home the sun is always shining.

It cannot have been easy for them having parents so far away, although they regularly assure me that this was an advantage. I can see it was also a relief for them having us absent for parent–teacher meetings, but it was also heartbreaking when we were not there for the triumphant rugby match or anniversary concert.

There will always be dodgy moments. The eleven-year-old waking in the night sobbing because she does not want you to go abroad again. The jolt to my heart when I realized that Barnaby only unpacked his suitcase when he got back to school; at home he pulled things out of it as he needed them. There have been irreplaceable lost weekends, missed Sunday lunches and hugs in the night, which we shall never get back, but when we are together, life is fast, furious and full of love. It sometimes feels as if we have to pack a month's worth of family life into one half-term week.

It is when children reach their teens that things become tricky. Before that, probably up to the age of ten, bringing up children abroad is heaven. Home-help and babysitting is usually cheaper, and children are made more welcome than at home. Freddie and Barnaby would quite often be swept out of our arms by complete strangers and passed around and fussed over like two spaniel puppies. It helped that they were both very blonde, which caused much oohing and aahing in the Far East. I suspect that Barney misses all the fuss and is rather surprised that no one comments on his now unremarkable shag-pile.

People who actually choose to give birth in foreign countries have my utmost admiration, particularly if it is their first child. (Actually, I think that they are stark raving bonkers.) My elegant sister-in-law had her first baby, a fiery redhead, whilst living in Japan. Nobody spoke a word of English and it was only after things were too far down the line for a change of plan that she discovered that not only was any kind of pain relief missing from the menu, but that yelling was also not allowed. Her firstborn finally made her appearance in the middle of an enormous earthquake with bottles falling off shelves, equipment smashing to the floor and doctors rushing to wedge open the doors in case the building shifted and they jammed shut. We all wanted her to be called Eartha, but she ended up as Molly. At least her molten lava hair serves as a reminder.

One of the other problems of having a baby abroad is registering its arrival.

After Barney was born in Hong Kong, I found myself in a hot, humid 'Ministry for Arrivals other than by Land, Sea or Air', seated in front of a mean-looking Cantonese official with steamed-up glasses. He was wielding a large black fountain pen.

'What your husband do?' he demanded.

'He is a diplomat,' I replied.

The official sighed and rapped his pen sharply on the form in front of him. 'But what he actually DO?'

Indeed, I had often wondered, but I wasn't going to be bullied by this man. 'Well . . . he's a First Secretary,' I said with all the confidence of one who knows her place.

'Secretary? Huh!' The official sneered. He poked his glasses up his nose and wrote SECRETARY in large black capitals under the heading FATHER'S OCCUPATION.

'No, no,' I insisted. 'He's not a *secretary*, he's a *Civil Servant*.'

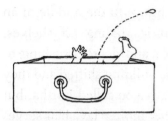

The official raised the corner of his upper lip in an even more contemptuous sneer, crossed out SECRETARY and wrote SERVANT.

Living abroad usually involves rented accommodation, and bringing up your toddlers in someone else's house amongst someone else's furniture is a luxury not to be underrated. Foreign-Office furniture is built to last and, by golly, it does. It is indestructible and adaptable. Both our children have slept in the top drawer of a Foreign Office-supplied chest of drawers. Emptied out, of course, and placed on the top, they make excellent cribs or nappy-changers, although coming from a family of four girls, I had no idea how far baby boys can pee when unrestricted. Somewhere there is a diplomatic family whose top drawer mysteriously smells of wee.

If furniture is indestructible, carpets are not. Our flat in Hong Kong was fitted throughout with beautiful, shiny wooden floors. The only exception was the drawing-room/dining-room, where a brand new cream carpet had been fitted. A week after moving in, when we were still unpacking our boxes and getting used to our new flat, I invited three children who lived downstairs to lunch. For a big flat the kitchen was minuscule and the only place to eat was the dining-room table, a hundred yards away down a slippery wooden corridor. I put the large bowl of greasy, hot, tomato spaghetti Bolognese sauce on my government-issue trolley and allowed the three children to push it down the corridor. What was I thinking of? I heard great whoops as the trolley gathered speed down the runway. It stopped abruptly as it hit the edge of the new cream carpet. The spaghetti continued into the middle of the white Axminster and lay there like a run-in with a snowplough in a ski resort.

TRAVEL TROUBLE

Any parent will tell you that it is not getting your assorted family members from A to B that is the problem; it is the logistical nightmare of keeping an eye on the teddy bear groupies and cute, cuddly camp-following stuffed toys which make up a child's vital support system. A child would quite happily mislay a parent, maybe two, but to lose a favourite toy is the end of their world. Barnaby attached himself to a huge, ugly brown bear which, to our excruciating embarrassment, he named Smeg. This beast was so large it was impossible to lose him, much as we often tried to at random railway stations or airports. He is still with us, at this very moment on Barnaby's bed surrounded by UCAS forms and back copies of *Zoo* magazine, leering at me with his remaining glass eye.

The love of young Freddie's life was a stuffed Panda, which, unlike Smeg, regularly got lost, resulting in the

sort of ferocious misery that only a small child can unleash. Panda went everywhere. He was so well travelled that we actually made him a very smart fake passport, full of jokes like 'the bear-er of this passport', etc. Customs officials all over the world solemnly stamped the appropriate page, while our serious five-year-old held the bear up for inspection. Indeed one of the most humiliating afternoons of my life was spent in the main Central underground station in Hong Kong holding Panda at arm's length inside the photo booth while I stayed out of shot outside, smiling pathetically at a queue of humourless Cantonese punters. Did these people not have Pandas that needed passport photos? What's more I had to do it twice as the bastard bear kept grinning.

Panda made his final break for freedom by staying behind in a Hong Kong taxi while the rest of us piled out for lunch at McDonald's. On realizing that Freddie's world was about to come to an abrupt end along with everyone else's in the restaurant, I shot off into the shopping mall

and discovered by unbelievable luck an exact copy on a World Wildlife Fund stall. I skidded back to McDonald's just in time to avert nuclear meltdown, and thrust the bright white-and-black new Panda into Freddie's arms.

'Bloody Panda, sneaked off for a new hair-do,' I said crossly. 'Don't give him any chips.'

The other mother I was with later gave me a ticking-off, saying that children 'had to learn to live with loss'. I reckoned that my children lived with loss anyway, having to move house every three years; it was hanging on to anything permanent that was the problem.

The ferociously organized sister-in-law has the best solution. She bought two of her children's favourite cuddly toys. One lived in a high cupboard. Every so often Lucy would swap them over, in order to even up wear and tear. When the inevitable loss occurred, life went on without a drama.

One useful tip when travelling long distances, particularly those that involve tedious waits at airports, is to tire children out, so that at least you can rest on the plane. We used to play a game called 'Dead Meat' in the airport lounge. You take with you an unloved, tatty soft toy, which you throw as far as you can, yelling 'Dead meat' as you do so. The child who retrieves the toy wins. This does not endear you to other passengers at first, but as other children join in, it can jolly up a journey no end.

The only thing worse than losing a favourite toy or

child is losing a passport. If a child feels it is grown-up enough to carry its own passport and hand it to the official for inspection, disabuse it immediately. Somehow in the confusion it will go missing.

In fact in over twenty years of shunting the family around the world we have only had one passport disaster and it wasn't entirely my fault. We were travelling around New Zealand in a camper-van. Charlie, who sees passport thieves behind every bush, had hidden our money and passports in the microwave, thinking that it looked vaguely like a hotel safe. I thought that I had removed everything before shoving in the potatoes and giving them ten minutes on full power, but hey – everyone makes mistakes.

The odd thing about microwaving a passport is that it emerges completely unscathed apart from one rather important thing: the photograph. Barnaby's photograph seemed to have melted and all his features, still discernible, had moved around his face into the wrong positions. Instead of my handsome boy, I had a Martian mutant with one huge eye in the middle of his face and an ear for a nose.

On returning to Hong Kong we explained to the Cantonese immigration officer what had happened. Stony-faced, he took the passport away to his superior's office and closed the door. Seconds later we heard gales of laughter and raucous Cantonese coming out of the room. Then the officer returned, not a flicker of a smile, and in

normal Cantonese English, which is devoid of all conso-
nants, told us that we could proceed. We could see him
checking Barnaby out though, counting his eyes, just in
case.

When you apply to replace a lost document, you have
to state the reason or circumstances under which the
old one was lost. Charlie had to write: 'microwaved by
mistake'.

CHILDREN'S PARTIES

Throwing a children's party abroad is a hit-and-miss
affair. For a start, the children will be a mix of nationalities
with different expectations, different likes and dislikes,
and will be wearing very different clothes. Far Eastern
children always arrive in pristine, elaborate party togs,
while a British child's idea of party wear is anything they
happen to be wearing at the time, be it pyjamas or, in the
case of one bold young man, not much at all.

I once organized a scavenger hunt on a Hong Kong
beach for one of the children's birthdays. I had to call a
halt quite quickly, as pretty little girls in pink party frocks
tiptoed through the mud to bring me used hypodermic
syringes and old condoms instead of the shells and driftwood I had been expecting. But this was as nothing
compared with the poor woman who organized a Pirate
Party on one of Hong Kong's smaller islands. The children

 were taken on an old wooden junk to a tiny tucked-away beach, where the main game of the afternoon was to be the 'discovery' of the hidden treasure – a huge papier-mâché Chinese vase filled with sweets. Unbeknownst to the lady organizer, behind an outcrop of rock at the far end of the beach was an ancient Chinese burial ground full of real Chinese urns, containing the cremated remains of venerated ancestors. Hordes of over-excited children happily emptied the burial ground of all the funeral urns, dragging them back across the sand to the appalled hostess, scattering remains as they went. They were a bit disappointed, it has to be said, when the urns proved to contain fag ash instead of the promised lemon sherbets.

Cultural differences are minefields. Our Argentinean friend in Peking decided that for his daughter's birthday party he would put on a real English Punch and Judy show. He had spent weeks building a puppet theatre and drafted me in to help, because he wanted it to be as authentic as possible, and he needed help with the voices. He had read up extensively and, as ever, the plot required Punch to be rather horrible to Judy. It was at this stage of the play, children spellbound, the puppet masters gaining in confidence, that Mr Punch had to start vigorously laying into Judy with his cudgel. Up jumped Teddy Mann, son of American journalist Jim Mann, grabbed Punch and wrestled him to the ground, yelling: 'Leave her alone, you bastard!'

There was a stunned silence. Teddy stood triumphant, his foot firmly on Mr Punch's head. Then the other children, roaring their approval, queued up for their turn to smash poor Punch to a pulp. Time for tea.

It is not only birthday parties where the unexpected can happen. International events can get competitive. Witness the Olympics. In one post, the primary school headmaster decided to host an International Food Festival. Everyone was to bring an example of their favourite national dish; food and wine was to be shared, and a mutual feeling of goodwill would spread through the assembled parents.

A good idea? Wrong. Never introduce national pride into an event: it is a recipe for disaster. It was an English mother who was the catalyst. Built along the same lines as a large male silverback, she made Les Dawson look like Claudia Schiffer. Her favourite pastime was hitching up her clothing to show you the miraculous results of her recent liposuction operations. In a strong Doncaster accent and with a voice grating like tin cans in a cement-mixer, she would pour out the grisly details: 'One and a half litres, one and a half litres of fat they sucked out of that,' she would growl, rubbing her still not insubstantial gut. 'Look at me now – flat as a board.'

She spent the Food Festival evening happily trotting

around pronouncing everything except her shepherd's pie 'absolutely bloody disgusting'. On taking one look at the Mexican Ambassadress's rabbit in chocolate sauce (a recipe of which she was inordinately proud) Mrs Flat as a Board screeched with laughter and announced to the playground: 'Eat it? I wouldn't even tread in it!'

Things were livening up nicely. A couple more of her critiques and others began to retaliate. Insults about each nation's culinary expertise and eating habits began to be swapped with gusto. The Mexican Ambassadress snatched up her *lapin molé* and stormed off, taking Brazil, Argentina and Uruguay with her. Glorious umbrage was taken by all as national dishes were snatched from under the noses of the unappreciative. The more Easterly Europeans retreated to their corner refusing to pass round their pork and dumplings, while France and Germany desperately offered sophisticated canapés, as they tried to calm things down. China vetoed everything in an effort to get to the puddings first.

But the best was yet to come. Tempers continued to simmer overnight. It appeared that some of Mrs Flat as a Board's rude remarks about the standard of cuisine had, as the evening progressed, strayed from the culinary to the more sexually explicit. Many of the ladies found out a few more unsavoury facts than they really needed to know about the true nature of their husbands' late-night conference calls. The following morning, one such lady, still fuming, rugby-tackled and then threw a tremendous punch at the lady from Doncaster. The two women lay sprawled on the ground flailing at each other until the gentle headmaster ('Please, ladies, not in front of the children!') finally managed to separate them: they'd been a bit like Oliver Reed and Alan Bates but with clothes on and not as pretty to look at.

TRAVELLING WITH TEENAGERS

I love teenagers. They sweep through your life and empty your fridge. As your children grow, so do your adventures as you get sucked into situations which would never have occurred had it not been for the presence of gawky fifteen-year-olds, who do not know the rules, or, like other essential items, have left them at home.

We have found that the best way to maintain peace and harmony in the holidays is to ship out as many of our children's friends as we could to wherever we were living at the time. There is no safety in numbers, but there is certainly more fun. We hid the vodka and the matches, borrowed camp-beds, turned all the bedrooms into

Mallory Tower-style dormitories and did not enter them again until the autumn, when we went in armed with a bottle of disinfectant.

Trips to the beach in Cyprus were always popular, although modern youth seemed less inclined to rough it in a mass camp-out under the stars. Admittedly the eight young males we took had been out all of the night before to a 'coffee shop' in Nicosia and on the way home had stumbled across a 'Foam Bar'. This was a new concept to me – some sort of seedy night-club filled with bubbles, frequented by well-oiled Greek gentlemen wearing nothing but skimpy speedos. Into this large bubble bath plunged eight of our young male house guests. Looking on the bright side, it was the only time they went any-where near soap during the entire holiday.

The boys were feeling frail when we took them to camp on the beach. By nightfall one or two had insufficient energy to blow up their airbeds and simply collapsed on the sand, their life support iPods firmly wedged in their ears to hide the sound of the mosquitoes. On setting up camp we discovered that one of the double airbeds would not inflate, so leaving the hunter-gatherer to deal with the fire and the sausages, I took Louis, perhaps more used to foam bars than some of the others and therefore still able to speak, off in my little open-topped car to see a Kurdish friend down the coast in the hope that he might be able to fix it. Louis was terrific company and we sat watching the

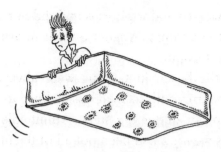

sun go down over a deserted North Cyprus coast, while Mashala took our mattress away to fix it.

Unfortunately, the only way he could manage this was to blow it up and seal the valve, so Louis and I were stuck with a tiny sports car, a king-size fully inflated airbed and five miles of empty dirt road. I drove very slowly with the mattress over my head, while Louis lay spread-eagled on top. It worked so well that every now and then I would get a little cocky and, as my speed rose, so did Louis and the mattress. Louis, at risk of floating away and landing in the wild thyme bushes by the side of the road, would yell, remarkably calmly I thought given the circumstances, and I would reduce my speed until he landed back on top of the car.

When Louis's mother later asked how his trip to Cyprus had gone, he did not mention the airbed, but he did say that it had been so hot on the drive back from the beach that he had had to put his book between his thigh and that of the boy next to him. 'Do you know, Mum,' he said, 'the sweat soaked all the way through to page 39?'

You cannot take your eyes off boys for a minute. I remember waking up in Libya at three o'clock in the morning and hearing strange sounds coming from the roof terrace. On going up the stairs in my nightie, I found Barnaby and two of his friends firing eggs at a nearby house with a three-man catapult. The house, huge and still under construction, although already partly inhabited, was rumoured to belong to a man with a dubious past.

Girls are much easier to have to stay. They are more helpful, they wash more, are surprisingly less picky, but they do attract groups of stray local males, who hang around like rejected spaniels. In Syria, Freddie said that they did not pinch your bottom so much as rub it like an Aladdin's lamp. Freddie's friend Kitty, who is beautiful, blonde and statuesque, and who comes to stay every summer, caused such a stir in Libya that she would find telephone numbers stuffed into her pockets, when she got home at night. When she, Freddie and Lavinia, another pocket Venus, were walking through the Medina in Tripoli, I had to walk a pace behind them growling like a dog at any overly bold chancer who came too close.

Girls are also more confident and outgoing. After Freddie finished her A levels she brought out a crowd of her girl friends to Cyprus to celebrate. They were the most beautiful and talented group of girls I have ever come across. There was an audible silence when they

used to sashay out of the changing rooms at the UN swimming pool, wearing not much more than their smiles.

On their first evening in Nicosia I planned a dinner party for them on a long table outside in the garden under the lemon and olive trees. I had covered everything with fairy lights and candles. The benefit of having a British regiment stationed nearby is that, within reason, the Commanding Officer is always willing to help out, in this case by supplying eight well scrubbed and mannered young men who arrived on the dot of eight, smartly turned out and carrying a large bunch of flowers. The evening was a roaring success. My favourite moment came when, carrying through the coffee, I overheard Amanda chatting to the shy young officer on her right. Amanda has a brain the size of a county, speaks Mandarin, does Maths Olympics for fun and is both charming, quirky and poetic. You never know what is coming next with Amanda. Nor did the shy young officer. 'You mean when you look at an open fig like that,' she said pointing to the fruit-bowl, 'you don't immediately think of a vagina?'

'No!' squeaked the poor boy, blushing to the roots of his hair.

His more robust companion did though. 'Never think of anything else,' he replied happily, to the cheers of his companions.

That summer Lavinia stayed on, and because she and

Freddie love drawing, I arranged for a model from my evening art class to come over one night and pose for us. The model was a voluptuous Cypriot lady with a well-rounded figure which was a joy to draw. She would stand for hours quite happy as long as she could wear her high, marabou-trimmed kitten heels and smoke.

The first evening Gula arrived very late and in a tizz, because on the way over she had rear-ended the car in front and crumpled her husband's pride and joy. Like most Cypriots she had been texting, smoking and checking her make-up at the same time and so could hardly be expected to have seen the traffic lights or the brake lights in front of her. Charlie and Barney were banished to the kitchen for the two hours we had booked her and the drawing class got under way, Gula standing resplendent in her kitten heels, merrily puffing away on a fag. But when the time came for us to put away our pencils and for Gula to put away her fine physique, she refused: her husband would be angry about the car. 'I no go home,' she declared.

Charlie and Barney were beginning to scratch at the kitchen door like a pair of Labradors in need of a lamp-post. The occasional attempt to bolt for freedom was repelled by their English modesty, which wilted in the face and embonpoint of an agitated Greek lady, striding around the house, flicking her ash and hair about and absolutely refusing to be cajoled into getting dressed. Finally Charlie hissed at me that he was damned well going to have his supper with the family in the dining-room and, if a naked Cypriot wished to join us, he was prepared to risk it. Gula eventually calmed down and left for home. Barney thought that she was marvellous. It was the nearest he has ever got to showing any interest in art.

HOME OR AWAY?

Looking back on the chaotic maelstrom that has been Freddie's and Barney's childhoods, although I would have loved to have been there for more of it as it passes so quickly, I'm not sure I would have changed any of the bits we shared. When the two of them were growing up they swore that they would never live abroad when they were older, but now, on the brink of leaving home, they are turning their faces towards jobs that will send them around the world. Perhaps it is because Charlie and I will be coming back to England permanently and they cannot stand the thought of that repeated Sunday-lunch summons. (Perhaps my cooking is worse than I had thought.)

They have ended up very close, which overseas siblings often seem to do, and will always call each other to check in. The other day Freddie told me that Barney had rung her from boarding school. It had been snowing heavily and he was telling her of the mayhem this had caused with great glee. Suddenly his mood changed and he swore fruitily down the phone. 'What's up?' asked Freddie.

'The bastards have made a snowman,' he replied gloomily.

'What's wrong with that?'

'It's on my bed.'

Every parent will have a cupboard full of brilliant childhood family memories which they can take out and warm their feet on on a miserable day. Ours are no different, just a little further afield and perhaps a little more exotic. Freddie galloping at full tilt through Petra on her camel with all the Bedouin stall-holders whooping and ululating. Blonde hair streaming out behind her, she skidded to a halt outside the Treasury, sliding off her camel triumphantly to the delight of the Arabs, who had dared her to do it in the first place.

Or Barnaby in Syria, bored to death while we looked around a Bronze Age burial site, sloping off with his friends Harry and Olly and, using a couple of old Coke cans as the goals, starting an impromptu game of rugby with the local boys, none of whom understood the intricacies of the rules. But somehow there emerged a Syrian set of laws and a wonderful game followed complete with scrums, tap-tackles and other things mothers shut their eyes at. Watching young men from completely different backgrounds, with no common language, communicate so successfully and happily was better than any dry burial mound and perhaps, just perhaps, gives some comfort in a hate-filled world.

Of course, the trouble with diplomatic offspring is that when they finally manage to spend a summer at home they often go a little mad.

The summer after Barney's GCSEs we found ourselves between postings with two months to enjoy a hot, sleepy, rather empty London.

Barney spent a lot of the time with the son of another diplomat who, like us, had failed to organise a summer holiday. They spent their time getting up to no good and sleeping over on various sofas.

One morning he arrived home looking sheepish, shifty and definitely the worse for wear. Having inadvisedly wandered downwind, I demanded the immediate removal of his T-shirt and jeans before we all had to move house. To my horror I saw that his torso was covered in deep scratches – but mysteriously his clothes were undamaged.

'Barney,' I asked warily, 'why are you covered in scratches?'

He looked at the ceiling and thought for a while, but realized he was cornered.

'I bumped into a large thorn bush,' he said slowly.

'So why,' I continued, 'aren't your clothes ripped?'

'That, Mum, would be because I wasn't wearing any.'

I kept calm. 'Barney,' I persevered, 'where was this thorn bush?'

'Wandsworth Common. But honestly, it was nowhere near the road – it was right out in the middle . . .'

'You were naked in the middle of Wandsworth Common,' I repeated dully. 'When?'

'Mum . . . it was a full moon! It was the middle of the night!' He spluttered. 'We were celebrating the end of exams. We just thought we'd take our clothes off and dance round a bit . . .'

'So what in God's name induced you to jump naked into a large bramble patch?'

He hesitated. 'Ahhh. That would have been the arrival of the squad car.'

I spent the next hour digging thorns out of my son's bottom with a hot needle. I was not kind. I was not gentle. And if I ever meet the policeman who, in the middle of the night, in the middle of Wandsworth Common, placed his size-eleven boot on a pile of Abercrombie and Fitch and said, 'Come out, lads! I've got your clothes – and I've got all night . . .' I'll buy him a drink.

There are, of course, a few truly bleak moments when living abroad; times when you are simply in the wrong place and at the wrong time. When the son of dear friends finally succumbed to leukaemia, we were travelling in West Africa and didn't get the terrible news until the day of the funeral, by which time it was too late to get home.

Instead we built a great fire out of driftwood on an empty Libyan beach and sat around it with our memories, while the sun slowly disappeared below the horizon. And so, on a distant seashore in North Africa, we raised our glasses and toasted that brave boy on his biggest journey of all.

7
Health Abroad

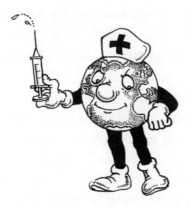

Never accept a lobster from a Somali.
(Advice from a young diplomat following forced evacuation in at
least three senses)

Bugs, beasts, and botulism

DOCTORS ABROAD

Foreign doctors can kill you. If you are still able to move
your arms and legs and wave your credit card, get yourself to an airline check-in desk as fast as you can. I know
that there will be people out there who will have had marvellous experiences: people who have had appendectomies

in a Mongolian yurt; who have been sewn up with a whale tooth and yak pubic hair and who were out riding across the plains two hours later. But on the whole, I would advise against it. There is nothing more miserable than being ill abroad. By the time you have learnt the words for 'You are joking. That thing is the size of an Exocet missile and it's not going up my . . .' it will already be nestling up nicely next to your last meal.

For every excellent doctor abroad I sometimes think there are two who downloaded their qualifications during a bored afternoon in a Benghazi internet café. Charlie and I once came across a sign in down-town Colombo for the 'Yelling Dental Clinic'. Perhaps it was so called because Sri Lankan dentistry must be made all the more complicated by the fact that nodding and shaking your head seem to mean the opposite of what we assume in Europe. So when that 1950s blunt industrial drill is poised over your throbbing tooth and the dentist asks if you would like pain relief, stick to the thumbs-up. Unless, of course, you are in Afghanistan, where the thumbs-up sign refers to an activity not usually associated with diplomacy, although quite often with diplomats.

Unfortunately, more often than not, when vital body parts let you down, flight is not an option and action must be taken wherever your medical misfortune has developed.

Our own catalogue of disasters include undiagnosed Lyme disease from Croatia, a nasty brain virus in Greece, giardia from New Zealand, dog-bites, monkey-bites, spider-bites and some exotic amoebae from Afghanistan with euphonious names but cacophonous effects and which seem to continue lurking in some forgotten colon that is forever England.

My first experience outside the NHS was in Greece. Charlie, like the inhabitants of Samuel Butler's *Erewhon*, tends to regard sickness as a crime, so he must have committed some capital offence in finding himself in a Greek hospital because his brain was hurting. It was the mid 1970s and all medication was administered by the next of kin. Painkillers came in suppository form, and his mother was a thousand miles away. I am not sure who was the more tense, he or I. Perhaps he was, because although I was perhaps not forceful enough, he clenched his squash-honed gluteus maximus and the suppository shot across the room like a ping-pong ball in a Thai brothel. I did not know the Greek for 'this suppository is covered in dust' and I had not heard of MRSA, so I gave it a wipe, let out a loud Hippocratic oath and rammed it home. I avoided finger-food for weeks afterwards.

Sometimes travellers would prefer to administer the medicine themselves. I will never forget a poor girl who turned up one day at the embassy in China in a pretty poor state. She had collapsed while travelling in the far western province of Xinjiang and had been carted off to hospital unconscious, dehydrated and feverish.

She had been roused from her unconscious state by the tortured wailings and moanings of someone in the bed next to her. On opening her eyes, she discovered that the source of the noise was a large, grey donkey tethered to the foot of its owner's bed. The doctor, when he finally arrived after finishing his noodles, most of which were down his front, picked up a syringe from the windowsill, wiped it upon his sleeve and jammed it into her main artery. At the first opportunity the poor girl ripped out her drip, grabbed her clothes, gave her medical chart to the donkey and headed for the embassy as fast as she could.

DOC-U-DRAMAS

When I first arrived in Cyprus, before I had had time to find my way around, I found myself in need of a little mundane medical help. Wandering around the old city, I suddenly came across a rather bashed-up old door with a sign saying 'Urologist'. Knowing that this was what I required, it being a recurrent problem, I knocked and went inside.

Surrounded by piles of old books, hundreds of impressive diplomas and shelf upon shelf of old marmalade jars filled with what looked like wiggly white olives, sat an old gentleman in a black suit and wearing a tie. Having sorted me out in an instant with a prescription, we sat and talked, there being no rush on my part and an empty waiting room on his. He explained that he had retired years before, but had been so bored at home he had taken to returning to his surgery on the quiet and seeing whoever wandered in through his doors of an afternoon. He was a charming man. As I got up to leave, I pointed to the old marmalade jars and asked him about the wiggly white olives. 'Those,' he replied in that rather sad Cypriot way, 'those are all prostate glands. In my time I have removed the prostate glands of almost every member of the Greek Cypriot parliament.'

He waved his long fingers rather lovingly over all the jars. 'They are all there,' he said, tapping one jar with his fingernail. 'Can I help you with anything else?' I have to say that for the four years we lived in Nicosia I never heard one whisper of sexual scandal concerning a Cypriot politician. Many concerning Archbishops, but perhaps they went to a different doctor.

After a few months I transferred to a delightful lady doctor, who, although her surgery was less atmospheric, was a little more up to date. She was also so indiscreet that it was a joy going to her for a consultation. On one visit she told me with great glee that she had just seen a female patient who was so rigorously clean and so religiously penitential that she scrubbed her bottom every morning, inside and out, with a hard toothbrush. On another occasion she told me of a patient, recently widowed, who had broken out in an agonizing rash after his new girlfriend had persuaded him to wax his testicles.

Cyprus, and in particular Nicosia, was so tiny that it was possible with a few well-aimed and seemingly innocent questions to work out who everyone mentioned was, which meant that going to diplomatic parties and watching who sat down gingerly was always interesting.

The only other doctor I had cause to call on in Cyprus was after I had been bitten by a wild dog whilst walking in the Green Line zone, the empty strip of land which is patrolled by the UN in order to keep the Turkish-Cypriot North and the Greek-Cypriot South apart.

It had been a long, hot and painful day, so when the doctor asked whether the dog had been Greek or Turkish, I am ashamed to say that I lost my temper. I said that I had no idea which side the dog came from; he hadn't bothered to talk to me since his mouth had been full at the time, and it didn't matter which side the bloody thing favoured anyway, because the fact that the sodding mutt had bitten me at all was obviously the fault of the perfidious British.

Surprisingly, he burst out laughing. He gave me a tetanus jab, but said that I wouldn't need rabies injections. He refused point-blank to take any payment. 'After all,' he

said, 'whichever way you look at it, you were bitten by a bloody rude Cypriot dog.'

At least doctors in Cyprus were easy to get hold of and you had a reasonably large selection to choose from. In China, if you needed to see a medic, there was only Dr Hartwig (or Earwig, as he was affectionately known). A rather robust Australian with a blunt turn of phrase and even blunter surgical instruments, he once attacked a particularly stubborn verruca, which had taken up residence in my left foot, with what seemed to be an electric carving knife. It was like Passchendaele. Unfortunately this particular visit to Earwig's abattoir coincided with the annual evening bash given by the exiled Cambodian Prince Sihanouk. This was always a lavish, if bizarre, affair. Why an exiled royal prince was giving a ball paid for by a communist government in an old Imperial Legation building for an assortment of bourgeois diplomats and journalists was beyond me, but it was an occasion not to be missed.

By the time Charlie and I arrived, late as usual, the party was in full swing. The diminutive Prince had just begun his speech of thanks and was in the middle of toasting all the brave journalists and aid workers who were risking life and limb to bring news of his unhappy and besieged country to the outside world. It was at exactly this point that we entered the enormous ballroom – me bravely leaning on Charlie's arm with my butchered right foot wrapped in white bandages flecked with blood, just back from Cambodia, having stepped on a land-mine . . .

The Prince paused, mid-eulogy. Ever a man for the dramatic gesture, he realized that a *coup de théâtre* had just plopped into his lap like an Air New Zealand stewardess. The tiny Prince minced towards me across the ballroom floor, microphone in hand and a look of heart-breaking concern on his face. 'Like this brave woman, so badly injured in the line of duty,' he sang out, his voice cracking with emotion.

He took my arm from Charlie and limped me slowly across the floor in front of all my journalist friends, who knew for a fact that the most dangerous thing I ever did was to eat yoghurt a week past its sell-by date.

The evening progressed downhill happily after this, with me ensconced on the table of honour. Charlie spent his time at an unobtrusive distance, occasionally exercising his limited skills in mime to indicate his delight at my predicament. Meanwhile the plump little Prince crooned his way through the evening, singing in over fourteen different languages throughout the night, with a furball of a grumpy Pekinese under his arm and his butterfly collection of wives and daughters swaying and beaming behind him. As a wounded war hero, I was excused joining in the conga and got away early at midnight, just as he was switching to Frank Sinatra and the odd Petula Clark number. As I limped off, past all the journalists and war correspondents cross-eyed with boredom, I wanted to say, 'Forget your war wounds, suckers. Get a verruca!'

WOMEN'S WOES

There are times when a woman only wants to see a woman doctor; times when only another woman could possibly empathize with all the quirks, rumbling and kinks that make up female plumbing.

Unfortunately, doctors abroad are not normally known for their innate sensitivity and understanding. In fact many seem to have been struck off at the point of origin. One South African doctor in Libya, before I had even sat down, told me in his thick Afrikaans accent that women only had two problems: 'hormones and more moans'.

I only had sore thumbs. He was so awful that I made Charlie come with me on my next visit. (He is after all a

lover of the absurd.) Ignoring me completely, he leant over to Charlie and, muttering conspiratorially, but quite audibly, said, 'Women are like cars. There comes a time when you should trade them in for a new model.'

In China, the only female medic in town was Ruth, the overworked embassy nurse, who ran a tiny clinic hidden away at the rear of the Chancery section. Officially she was there to look after the embassy staff – unofficially she looked after most of the foreign community.

It was not too long after the Falklands war, and the Foreign Office had sent out instructions to all its embassies to have nothing to do with our Argentinean opposite numbers. In their embassy at the time was a sweet woman, wife of one of the junior diplomats, and beloved by us all. We became aware that something was worrying her, and she became more and more silent and unhappy. Eventually we winkled it out of her that it was a medical problem that was weighing her down and that she urgently needed to speak to a woman doctor. Ruth was the answer, but Argentineans were forbidden to enter our embassy. This was, of course, nonsense, as we all got on rather well. In fact, the Argentinean ambassador with his sports-jackets and pipe looked more English than ours did.

In the end we wrapped her up in blankets – it was winter – and shoved her in the back of a car boot before driving her through the embassy gates. Smiling merrily at the ex-British servicemen guards, we parked round the back and pulled her out of the boot and into Ruth's room. It all turned out well, and later on, having smuggled her out

_ya....natürlich.
I alvays sunbaze
in ze nude.....
Jutht as Nietzsche
intended.

THE
GERMAN
CULTURAL
ATTACHÉ

again and celebrating over a glass of wine, we decided that women sticking together took priority over things like war, and that in future we should all buy cars with large boots.

On a more delicate note, in a surprising number of countries it is impossible to buy tampons, which can sometimes adversely colour your first impressions of a place. Before we left for Peking, I went round John Lewis with Charlie to buy all the things we had been told were unavailable in China, sufficient to last us for three years. I had filled up two trolleys with make-up, toiletries and tampons, and had left Charlie to guard them while I searched for something else. A very senior Foreign Office colleague happened to pass by, looked at the stack of tampons, raised an eyebrow at Charlie and passed on without a word.

A friend and her husband were being thrown out of Moscow in one of those periodic and tedious tit-for-tat spats. They were being escorted towards the Finnish border when she had to call a halt and dive into the shrubbery. To her horror as she entered the thicket, she realized that she was to be accompanied every inch of the way by four burly KGB officers, who had no intention of turning their backs but were to witness all the ins and outs of this delicate matter, presumably in case she was burying a secret message. After such an indignity French lavatories are a doddle.

KEEPING FIT

There is no excuse for not keeping fit abroad. I have had all types of physical activity thrust upon me in any number of places and, thank God, I have managed to abandon them all.

I have tried tap-dancing in Hong Kong; a variety of Romanian boxing where we had to yell 'KILL' very loudly and regularly, which upset the Bible Study Group upstairs; and a 'Discover Inner Harmony through Dance' class, which was apparently all the rage in Italy, but proved completely unsuitable for the more down-to-earth and vulgar British. I have also attended yoga classes all over the world, although I recommend avoiding these in places where chickpeas and hummus constitute a major part of the diet.

In Cyprus the unfair amount of sunshine and the location of my house next to some courts meant that tennis was the torture of choice among my friends. We would often meet in the evening, enjoy a glass of wine and then play. One evening after a slightly longer wine prelude than normal, I found myself consistently failing to hit a single shot. It was not until I tried to serve under the inadequate lights that I realized that I was trying to play with a racquet that had no strings at all. It was scary how long it took me to notice.

One glorious weekend the military attaché decided to organize a tennis tournament. Realizing that he didn't have enough players to make his complicated rota work, he applied to the colonel in charge of the Green Line dividing Cyprus to send over some troops to make up the numbers. In true army fashion, instead of asking which of the soldiers actually played tennis, the officer in charge just picked out the four nearest, three of whom had never held a tennis racket before. One poor girl, a Royal Artillery officer, was paired up with an Argentinean of near-professional standard. She said it was more frightening than serving in Basra.

In Libya I occasionally attended a 'mixed' aerobic class. Nothing is mixed in Libya. People never meet the opposite sex, except when they marry or have a car crash. But the beautiful Lindsay from the embassy had given me such outrageous descriptions of veiled women in long track suits sweating it out with large Arab men in 'wife-beater' T-shirts that I had to go along to check them out myself. It was true, and brutal. A Palestinian army captain, with biceps like brown cannonballs and buttocks which could crack walnuts, screamed his way around the class, towel-whipping the men into frenzies of action, bellowing into the women's ears until at least fifty more tummy-tucks were completed. Just when you thought that you had stepped into a scene from *Midnight Express*, the tempo changed entirely and Captain Macho had his arms above his head and was wiggling his hips. It was then that I realized that all the men had shaved their armpits. My fear of

the gym Gauleiter disappeared: how can you be scared of a man once you have a vision of him standing in the shower fiddling with his Lady Shave.

MASSAGES

I cannot make up my mind whether I am a fan of massage or not. As a general rule, in Arab countries you can be sure that it is all done in a spirit of health and well-being. On the days the Hamams are open to women, everyone seems to be having a party, but in the nude. It is rather exhilarating and innocent. Charlie and Barney tell me that their Hamam sessions in Damascus, set in some old Ottoman baths, were much calmer and very civilized.

In Europe and Asia you have to be more careful. I once spent a glorious afternoon with my friend Susie in the recently restored Hamam on the Greek-Cypriot side of Nicosia. We happily baked ourselves on hot stones and braised ourselves in steam. Later we opted for a massage administered by a very good-looking Russian masseur, brought in specially from Moscow. It all seemed to me to be a bit near the knuckle, or rather, the knuckle seemed to be a bit close to my business end. Susie and I wondered whether it was normal or not, but, being British, shook the masseur by the hand and thanked him profusely. (Abroad

I tend not to question things too much.) Two weeks later Susie rang. Had I read in the paper that the Russian masseur had been sacked and sent back to Moscow for inappropriate behaviour in the massage cubicle?

The Hamam on the Turkish side was a far scarier proposition. It was much older and scruffier. I didn't dare to chance the huge, bald Turk who ran it, who oiled his body and probably tortured people on Saturdays. Charlie's predecessor did, after a dare on a drunken evening. Apparently he emerged in one piece, shining and pink, about two hours later. 'It was fine,' he said softly. 'Fine. Until he lifted my manhood and scrubbed my testicles with a wire brush.'

Thank God I only had the Russian.

FOREIGN LOOS

Anyone setting off on a journey to strange places will have one question strong-arming its way to the front of the anxiety queue: what will the loos be like? Sleeping arrangements and pillows come a close second, but lavatories rank as the Big One. Is there a God? Why are we here? Will there be soft lavatory paper and a proper seat? The first two questions don't even get brain-space.

Let us be brutally honest. Performing *en plein air* is not my thing. I have been blessed with few physical talents and hunkering down in open spaces is at the top of my list of sporting activities to be avoided at all costs. In evolutionary terms I have left my cavewoman ancestors way behind: I am not built to squat.

For me, the problems of a looless landscape are almost insurmountable. I am a locked-door, drawn-curtains, cough-very-loudly type of girl. I am only really happy getting down to business if the fire alarm has just gone off and the whole area has been evacuated for at least a mile in every direction. How do women manage on boats? No wonder Ellen MacArthur sailed around the world single-handed.

Recently a group of us, including the ever-elegant sister-in-law, an even chicer friend, Peach, who came armed with a pile of *Vogue* and *Tatler* magazines, some family friends and two revolting teenage boys, wandered off deep into the Libyan desert. It was officially 'The Middle of Nowhere'. For seven days and nights we travelled through one of the emptiest and most beautiful places on earth, equipped with not much more than a sleeping-bag and a packet of wet wipes. Vague memories of lavatories we had once loved were irradiated away under the microwave desert sun and talk around the camp-fire at night lingered longingly over Jo Malone and extra-soft quilted. After three days of roaring up and down a thousand sand-dunes I was confident that with the wind behind me and a stiff upper lip I could hold out for the entire trip. Mother Nature, on the other hand, being the old bitch that she is, had other plans. With the dogged persistence of the Colditz escape committee my previous breakfasts insisted that I succumb to the inevitable.

There is no privacy in the desert. There are no trees or boulders. It takes half an hour to walk behind the nearest sand-dune. It is also completely impossible to saunter inconspicuously with a head torch, a trowel, four packets of wet wipes and a roll of loo paper on a string around your neck – and if you are my friend Peach, a copy of *Vogue*.

Once I had traversed miles of hostile terrain, checked the ground for scorpions, sand-vipers and sniggering teenagers with flash-bulbs, I faced down-wind and lowered the drawers and myself. Collapse of stout party. I had made the rookie error of not finding a flat sand-dune and had started facing uphill. Sand sticks to a bare bottom, I discovered. Nothing for it, I just had to grit my teeth as well and turn through 180 degrees.

It was extraordinary how each member of the group dealt with the problem in his or her own way. The ever-elegant sister-in-law got on with the job in her very British, no-nonsense fashion. Peach the Chic always took a magazine and her sunglasses in case she met someone she knew. The teenage boys opted for the group poop, accompanied by gales of laughter and lewd remarks, while Charlie treated it like a competition. He comes from a long line of whatever is the opposite of an anal retentive.

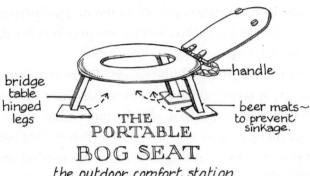

bridge table hinged legs — handle

THE
PORTABLE
BOG SEAT
the outdoor comfort station

beer mats~ to prevent sinkage.

His father at prep school in the thirties had to line up with the whole school every day. Each boy was marked out of five by matron and failure to pass a certain score led to a dose of syrup of figs.

Without doubt the greatest place for lavatorial disasters is China, although to be fair we lived there in the mid 1980s when it was still emerging from the dense red fog of Mao's great social experiment and things were still a little raw.

At that time if ever you got caught short in a public place and had to frequent a socialist squatter, or what Mr Blair would no doubt have called 'the People's loo', you would find yourself the victim of considerable unwelcome attention. Entertainment was thin on the ground. Not only would you be followed in by half the women in the street, but you would have to suffer the indignity of being closely inspected by local ladies bending over and staring at your waste disposal unit. As if that were not bad enough, they would then cackle with laughter, point out certain features of your plumbing to their friends, who then went to fetch the neighbours to join in the fun. I still have not worked out which particular part of my undercarriage merited such hilarity.

Once, in Mongolia, the lavatory I was in was *so* smelly that I almost fainted into a great open sewer running along the back, but luckily my brave friend Juliet rescued me in the nick of time by grabbing my lapels and hauling me, knickers still around my ankles, into the fresh air. It would have been a messy death.

The public loo in some of the more rural villages in China served several purposes. Recycling centre, for example. It was also the social hub of the community. Here gossip was passed on and news shared. A bit like Starbucks, but somewhat smellier and in reverse.

In post-Mao China, squatters were definitely still considered to be the vehicle of choice for good honest communists. The Chinese were not much taken with the capitalist running-dog seated variety and you would often find footprints on the seat where a good son or daughter of the revolution had resolutely followed the slogan's injunction to avoid bourgeois liberalism.

Perhaps this political rectitude and disdain for capitalist crappers is what lay behind the fate which befell the couple below us in the diplomatic ghetto in Peking, where all

ENTRENCHING
TOOL

HEAD TORCH

FISHING
WAISTCOAT

with 100 pockets
for holding
bathroom
accessories.

WET WIPES

in industrial
quantities.

LOO-ROLL
NECKLACE

an invention of
the author's to
keep hands free
for essential
business.

PLASTIC BAG

for refuse retrieval and,
in extreme circumstances,
ANONYMITY
although NEVER at the
same time.

STURDY BOOTS

for
spider-squashing
and
splash-back
situations

~THE~
AUTHOR'S OWN
OUTDOOR OFF-LOADING
ENSEMBLE

foreigners had to live. They had a cracked lavatory seat. All repairs had to be carried out by a plumber from the Chinese diplomatic service bureau. There was no choice, because it was next to impossible to buy anything in China at the time. Shaking his head sadly at the broken seat, the plumber told them that there were no more to be had in the whole of China. Resigned to spending the rest of their posting perched on an icy ceramic rim, they were about to show the gentleman to the door when he whipped out a large wooden mallet and with one swipe reduced the lavatory to a heap of shattered china fragments. Without the seat the lavatory was obviously useless, so he had decided to remove the old one altogether and order them a new one. 'How long will that take?' asked our friends nervously.

He shrugged. 'About a year,' he replied.

In China hygiene is definitely a state of mind. One frozen, ice-encrusted winter, we travelled to Harbin, a city near the Chinese–Russian border, where architecturally East and West tumbled over each other in a rag-tag of neglect. Where the crumbling onion domes of Orthodox churches stand frosted and peeling next to steam-pumping brick chimneys, and stately *belle époque* windows look down on the grey, coal-dust city, their broken panes patched and papered with yesterday's manifestos. On street corners men with rabbit-ear hats sold frozen rats held up by their frozen tails like grey, furry ice lollies. We were there for the winter ice-carving festival, when the frozen River Song is carved into dragons and pagodas, and screaming boys tear down man-made ice slides on metal trays, their breath rasping in clinker-filled clouds of frozen steam.

We had booked a room in the only hotel, famous for having blamed a huge fire the year before on a hapless foreigner who was accused of falling asleep while smoking in bed. Large signs all over the rooms read, 'NO SMOKING IN BED'. As all the ashtrays had been taken away, inevitably everyone dropped their cigarette butts all over the floor. More worrying, though, was the bathroom, where on top of the lavatory was a large sign in Chinese reading 'STERILIZED'. Beneath, in the bowl, bobbing happily, even impertinently, was something the size of a dugout canoe; not so much a French Malteser, as John Lloyd likes to call them, as *une roulade entière*. Charlie summoned the floor attendant. 'Excuse me,' he said in exquisite Mandarin, 'but could you tell me whether this turd was also sterilized when you did the lavatory?'

It remained, disinfected and sterilized. Perhaps it was a Chinese bugging device (rather a good place to hide it really, as it resolutely refused to go round the U-bend, even when helped on its way with the bog brush). It kept popping back up like a happy otter and remained with us for the whole weekend.

Not that one needs to go as far afield as China in order to experience a different view of hygiene; the French are none too hot either. I have had moments in French bathrooms, where frankly, if the smell does not kill you, the décor will.

By far my worst French lavatory moment occurred in a ski resort. Apart from the fact that I really *am* the woman who sneaked off-piste for a pee only to find herself sliding rather fast back on to the run, crouching like a ski jumper going the wrong way, the other mishap was far more distressing. We had met some friends in a very expensive restaurant in Meribel. As we are normally a 'sandwich on the lift' sort of family, I was feeling pretty grumpy anyway. The loo, of course, was pitch-black, freezing cold and hardly big enough to swing *un chat*. My jacket was bulky; the floor was slippery; my breath was steaming up my glasses and my gloves had fallen into an ominous puddle on the floor. And this being France there was, naturally, no lavatory paper. So I had to make do with some crunchy frozen tissues out of my pocket. It was only later, when the bill arrived, that I realized to my absolute horror, as I pulled some pristine tissues out of my other pocket, that I had just wiped my bottom on 80 Euros. A gesture worthy of the UK Independence Party, but I still find it hard to talk about.

It is quite an interesting facet of our national psyche that we goody-two-shoes British, who normally obey every dictat out of Brussels, were the only embassy in Cyprus which steadfastly disobeyed their national policy of 'no-lavatory-paper-down-the-loo'. The Superpower Americans all meekly filled the little silver loo-side dustbins, but the Brits simply refused. Bemused that a country with such antiquated plumbing could ever have been allowed into the EU, we stubbornly dropped the lot round the U-bend.

It is my opinion that the English suffer more than most when dealing with affairs of the bathroom, or *toilettage* as the French call it, but we deal with it stoically. Rise above it, I say – find music in your movements. In the words of Mick, the 'Sarf London' gentleman who swept our street in Clapham and made it his business to know every single resident and who or what they were up to: 'Vere's a professor lives darn ver ovver end of ver street,' he told me one day in his strangely attractive, Bob Hoskins-on-steroids accent. "E's been working for free years on his faeces.'

So it is not just me who is obsessed.

8

Visitors Abroad

*Guests can be, and often are, delightful, but they
should never be allowed to get the upper hand.*
(Elizabeth von Arnim)

Household infestations of a human kind

BE MY GUEST

In a quarter of a century of house-guestery, I have only once considered murder. Most of my guests have not only been fun, charming and usually house-trained, but I also find that when they have left, the house is horribly silent and empty without them. That longed-for moment when you can finally leap around your house stark naked, yelling like a banshee and dancing to the

Rolling Stones is never quite as much fun as you expected.

In Libya I longed for guests. I missed London so much that I was thrilled when London came to me. Every guest brought the house to life, and I was heartbroken when each one deserted me for the airport. Bugger the Visitor's Book: I wanted them all to sign the wall in the hall, but I wasn't sure how the Accommodation Officer would take it.

The pleasure of guests is spending time together. How often do you have the chance in England of more than a natter over supper or a quick exchange at the school gates? Having someone to stay allows you to deepen friendships and to forge new ones.

It hasn't all been plain sailing. I will admit to tense moments with drunken gap-year travellers, tooth-grinding annoyance with screaming infants . . . and to exasperation with the young man who blocked my lavatory after three weeks on the Trans-Siberian Express. The ravages of his Russian and Mongolian diet had clearly proved too much for the U-bend and he appeared to have baled into the bath, into the basin, into the bidet and out of the window with the zealous enthusiasm of a Lincolnshire muck-spreader.

There is an art to enjoying guests. The key is enthusiasm. Guests drag you off for adventures around town when you would otherwise be curled up at home with a

crossword; they make you revisit your surroundings and see the Forbidden City or the Medina through new eyes. They have usually studied the guide-books – something I never bother to do – and can not only take you to places you haven't seen before but also tell you what you are looking at when you get there. On the other hand, you must be careful to watch out for cultural overload. Sometimes guests just want to relax. When asked if he wanted to visit some Temple of Heavenly Effulgence or other, my father-in-law, a military man who often speaks in acronyms, replied that he was 'NAFT-ed, thank you'.

'NAFT-ed?'

'Yes. Not Another Fucking Temple.'

It has entered the family vocabulary as an all-purpose word to express the idea that you would rather stay at home.

PUTTING UP WITH PEOPLE YOU PUT UP

Just occasionally it is necessary for your sanity to take evasive action. I should perhaps have divorced Charlie for what he did with the Guest from Hell, but I just wished that I had thought of it first. On the last evening of her stay, she invited us both out to dinner. Charlie was thrilled, he said, but unfortunately he had an official dinner. So I had to suffer alone.

And suffer I did. Every restaurant I recommended was inadequate. One was too bright, another too dark; one too naff, another too glitzy. One, God forbid, only served Chinese food. In the end, I had had enough. By the time we arrived back at our apartment block I was on the edge of a nervous breakdown – not quite the nineteenth but getting close. I let the guest into the flat and lied that I had promised our colleagues downstairs that I would pop in on some errand.

I lay on the sofa in Tom and Kay's apartment, drink in hand, venting my wrath. It slowly dawned that there was something strange about their reactions: more amused than sympathetic. Then I noticed the armchair in the corner seemed to be shaking. I rose and with as much dignity as I could muster, crossed the room and pulled it back to reveal Charlie lying on the floor, tears of laughter pouring down his face. There was no official dinner; he had spent the evening with Tom and Kay, happily speculating on what purgatory I was going through. To this day I'm not sure whether I've forgiven him. There will surely be some special layer of a Dante-esque hell for men who cheat on their wives with an armchair.

Sometimes house guests like to tag along with us to official functions if they happen to coincide with their stay. They imagine that it is what diplomats spend their time doing and want to see if we really do dress in black tie and eat Ferrero Rocher chocs. In fact there is an art to attending these occasions: enter when most people are already there, eat as many shrimp balls as you can, clap loudly when the ambassador makes his speech and then sneak out of a back door.

If I like our guests sufficiently, I will introduce them to my Favourite Game. Diplomatic and expatriate communities have more than their fair share of bores. Charlie might be able to pretend to find a Finn's view on European monetary policy fascinating, but I can't. My tolerance reserves run dry notoriously quickly. Then I play Diplomatic Pass The Parcel.

There is no music and it is best not to unwrap anything. The idea is to nominate a Bore, engage him in conversation, then off-load him, ruthlessly, on to another Player whilst he is in full diplomatic flow. As with all serious sports, your position on the field of play is all-important. You must be facing the bulk of the crowd to maximize your off-loading potential. When your Bore is fired up and cruising on full throttle you begin to scan the room for a Player. Then, as the unfortunate victim unwittingly passes by, you grab them and say to the Bore: 'I am so sorry to interrupt, Excellency, but my friend Jo Fitz would be frightfully interested in what you are saying. She is an expert in Lithuanian chicken breeding.' This is followed by the killer blow: 'Jo, your glass is empty. Let me get you a refill.'

Fifteen love, as Jo glowers, powerless to return your

drop-shot. Of course, on the way to the bar, it's all too easy to take your eye off the ball. An old hand like Charlie will always seize a moment of weakness: 'Ah, Cherry,' (grabs elbow) 'have you met Mme Grospoitrine? She is deeply into handicrafts. I see you have an empty glass. Let me get you a refill.'

Fifteen all.

We had a lovely policeman, John, to stay in Cyprus. He was particularly keen to accompany us to a reception. I tried to warn him off, but he thought it might be fun. So in the car I briefed him on Diplomatic Pass the Parcel. I was not entirely convinced that he had grasped the concept, but we launched in anyway. At the reception I had the good luck almost immediately to bump into the most

boring man on the island. I introduced John, excused myself adroitly and watched progress from the other side of the room. Nothing happened. John stayed put. Every now and then I caught his eye and received a surreptitious thumbs-up in reply, but he still made no move to Pass the Parcel.

An hour or so later, I scooped John up, his face bug-eyed with forced attention, and headed for home. 'So did I do?' he asked eagerly. 'Did I break the record?'

'What record? You were supposed to pass him on! That's the point.'

'Oh,' said John, crestfallen. 'I missed that part. I thought it was to see who could stand him the longest.'

THE UNWELCOME GUEST

Unwelcome guests are incredibly rare; we have only ever had the one in twenty years. Tom and Kay Smith had a man to stay in Peking, who was so ghastly that after finally disposing of him at the airport, they returned home to crack open a bottle and celebrate his departure. Just as they were childishly jumping up and down on his bed, chanting 'The beast is gone!', they remembered that they had not locked the front door. When Tom went out to see to it, their guest was standing in the doorway watching them. He had left his passport and ticket on his bedside table and had taken a cab back from the airport to fetch them.

Our Guest from Hell came with a glass-shattering voice and the habit of yelling 'Hello, everybody!' in a high Shirley Temple screech. She kept sighing and asking if there was anything more interesting to do after we had dedicated an afternoon to showing her around an historic site which we had visited a hundred times before.

I like my guests to feel at home. But there is a limit. She would wander into our bedroom uninvited and rifle through our wardrobes.

One evening, after a dinner party, she yawned and declared that she would simply die if she had to spend time with boring people 'like that'. When I told her that these people were my friends, she patted my hand, looked at me with soulful eyes and said, 'Poor, poor you.' She lives on: it has become a family catchphrase.

My only advice to deal with guests who behave badly is alcohol, meditation or medication. If all else fails, try poisoning them. A good dose of laxative in the chocolate mousse can keep them in their rooms for at least three days.

OFFICIAL VISITORS

One of the more entertaining aspects of being attached to an embassy is meeting all the Official Visitors. The majority are male, and I have no objection to being asked to 'balance the numbers', or even to accompany the Minister's wife in her quest for silk underwear for her husband (a whole generation of Cabinet ministers in the mid eighties were kitted out by me). No, being used as gender ballast is just fine, as long as I get to be unleashed into the VIP enclosures. I am usually pleasantly surprised by the bureaucratic flotsam and jetsam which floats through embassies.

Although most people go out of their way to behave when they are on official business, one or two think it is an opportunity to be obnoxious and throw their weight around. It is a bit like haggis: a fine national dish in Scotland, but removed from its habitat it reverts to its true self; an old bladder stuffed with the floor sweepings from an abattoir. Some ministers and lofty officials would be better left in the charnel house of Westminster.

My experience, if I may generalize, has been that Labour politicians have been far better mannered than Conservatives, although I was very taken with one Tory Peer who had re-entered public life in the role of businessman, having resigned his government position as a result of a little imbroglio with a bevy of call-girls. Beaming bonhomie, he was sitting in the ambassador's garden taking coffee after lunch. It was spring and the lawn was knee-deep in white fluffy blossom, which was snowing from the trees. Her Majesty's Britannic Ambassador, who could occasionally lapse into pomposity, fluttered his hands over the coffee cups as the seedlings fell in clouds. 'I do apologize. Perhaps we should move inside,' I suggested.

'Oh,' replied his Lordship, 'don't worry. I am rather partial to a bit of fluff.' And he roared with laughter.

It was fascinating to see how some of the big guns matched up to their reputations. John Prescott called a press conference in Cyprus and opened it by saying how glad he was to be visiting Malta. Edward Heath was much more fun than I had expected and told endless, bitchy stories about Margaret Thatcher. James Callaghan was sweet and kind, like a favourite uncle. At an embassy buffet, we were getting along famously, discussing publishing. His memoirs were about to come out and I had a children's book in the pipeline. Suddenly I felt my elbow grasped and some oleaginous parliamentary minion whispered loudly in my ear: 'You were invited to entertain Mr Callaghan's bodyguard, NOT Mr Callaghan himself.'

I felt like an eighteenth-century trollop. 'Threepenny upright, Mr Callaghan? Oh, you're the bodyguard. In that case it'll be a penny.'

I never had the chance to meet Mrs Thatcher, but those who did were universally impressed by her ability to soak up information, order it and fire back penetrating questions. On one visit to China she was being briefed by a senior member of the embassy, when he realized to his horror that she was transfixed by the fluorescent Barbie-pink nail varnish which he had failed to remove after the embassy *Rocky Horror Show* party the night before. Mrs Thatcher said nothing: she probably considered it quite normal in Foreign Office circles.

Once or twice in your life you will have the misfortune to come across someone so malignant, they leave you breathless. The kind of people who weren't born; they were just dug up at midnight. About half-way through our Peking posting, Charlie drew the short straw of having to accompany a certain official around China, and I drew the even shorter straw of having to tag along to keep his wife company. She was certifiably insane. In her passport, under 'profession' she had written 'Peeress of the Realm', and she had declared it her mission to 'bring culture to China'. So much for three thousand years of poetry, painting, calligraphy and those silly pots, then. They had visited before and had only come back because 'the Chinese adore us'.

Things started fairly calmly in Peking. I was excused the welcoming banquet, but Charlie had to sit between the Peeress and a poor Chinese Minister's wife to interpret. He told me later that it was a surreal experience. He started off by translating comments such as: 'Do you have trouble passing laws in China?' – this, three years before the Chinese had no trouble in gunning down protestors in Tiananmen Square.

But when she asked whether the Minister's wife knew her dear friend Bertie and was surprised to hear that she did not, Charlie realized he was going to have to think on his feet.

'The Peeress says that she is so happy to be back in China,' he translated.

'When was she last here?' came out as 'No, she does not know Bertie, but she is sure that he is a fine fellow.'

'Bertie came to dinner last week and I told him he had to be firmer with the backbenchers' went back as 'Two years ago. We do so love China and the Chinese people.' They got on famously and parted with beaming smiles. Charlie came home ragged.

On the provincial part of the tour things started with a bang when the Peeress hit a Chinese air hostess over the head with her handbag because the flight had been delayed.

One minute the poor girl was doors to manual and the next she was grounded. Charlie, as the Chinese speaker, was despatched to sort out the flight, but unaccountably failed to clear fog in Shanghai a thousand kilometres away.

From then on, things not so much spiralled as plummeted. In Shanghai a delayed private dinner with the Consul General did not meet expectations. Admittedly the cook had come from the No. 4 Iron and Steel Factory and was more familiar with foundry than haute cuisine, but she was lucky to have been fed at all.

Meanwhile, our Chinese minders were also getting it in the neck. The Peeress, with her great love of China, developed a pathological distaste for poor Mr Tang, one of the interpreters. Perhaps it was his accent (he had spent fourteen years in Mali). We thought it was rather touching that a Chinese should sound exactly like a West African, but the Peeress did not. Of course, his frequent expectoration did not help. She banned him from her presence and shouted 'take him away', like the Queen of Hearts, every time he approached.

On the train to Hangzhou, poor Charlie had to sit in their compartment, while I sat in the next-door one, laughing and joking with the Chinese. In those days they always kept their distance in case anyone accused them of being pro-Western, but adversity does tend to unite. Every now and then I would go in next door, appear solicitous and pull a face surreptitiously at Charlie. The Peeress was on top form. On one occasion she looked out of the window as we passed a small, dilapidated village house and exclaimed, 'Just look at that. What a mess. Honestly, these Chinese! With a little effort that would make a fine second home.'

At Hangzhou the ghastly denouement came, inevitably. We were all to dine with the governor, his trade officials and other dignitaries of a province with a population the size of that of Germany. Her Ladyship was objectionable to everybody. Goaded beyond endurance I opened my mouth to give her some fruity convent-girl slang, and just in time Mr Tang rushed in and said he needed my passport. He dragged me outside and, unprecedented for a Chinese at that time and probably risking a long sentence in the Chinese gulags, he gave me a huge hug and said, 'She is bad, bad woman!' A little calmer, I rejoined the group as we were about to get into the lift and go down for the dinner. There was a further pause while the Chinese fixers asked Charlie something about next day. The Peeress flew off the handle at the delay, and ordered us all, including the Chinese interpreters, into the lift. As the doors closed she said, 'Those Chinese. They are like monkeys. They should be locked up in cages.'

Miss Wong, the chief interpreter, went red and looked at the floor. As their Lordships got out of the lift in the lobby, Charlie pressed the 'door close' button and, turning to the interpreters, said in Chinese that there was nothing

he could say in apology that was adequate; he was morti-
fied. Miss Wong claimed that she hadn't heard. But
Charlie knew that she had. Worse was to come.

At dinner, we were all seated around one large circular
table. For reasons lost in the Peeress's psyche she had
decided that only her husband, the Governor, herself and
the chief interpreter were allowed to speak. Charlie was
sitting next to a man with millions of dollars of contracts
in his back pocket to dole out to foreigners and was discussing business with him. The Peeress kept rapping the
table, barking out imperious instructions at everybody to
stop talking.

As this Mad Hatter's Tea Party started hotting up, Mr
Tang took his hollow, ceramic chopstick rest and, under
the table, filled it with matchstick heads, rolled up a paper
fuse, and lit it, murmuring to me, 'I blow woman up,
yes?'

'Yes,' I said happily.

The climax came with his Lordship's speech. The poor
interpreter on duty for the dinner was a nervous wreck.
Quite early on in the speech the poor man had translated
'China lacking vision' as 'having bad eyesight'. Charlie's
subsequent correction drove the Peeress into paroxysms
of table-rapping, with her shrill cries of 'QUIET! BE
QUIET!' effectively silencing the entire room. Her
husband, ignoring her outburst and the shocked faces of
the Chinese, continued with a long quotation from the

Book of Proverbs, to the bafflement of the Governor, whose communist education had not encompassed the study of the Bible. He turned to Charlie for help, who said to his Lordship, 'Excuse me, Lord X, but I do not think that the governor has understood your reference to the Book of Proverbs.'

'Of course he has!' his Lordship exploded. 'Everyone's read the Book of Proverbs. I've read the Book of Proverbs. The governor's read the Book of Proverbs.'

'QUIET! QUIET!' screeched his wife.

There are times when it is just wiser to furl the sails and run before the storm.

The only advice I can offer, should you ever be faced with a VIP or CEO who insists on behaving badly on an official visit, is Be Prepared. Smile, breathe deeply and keep calm. Or you could try the old British Airways trick of being very polite in a wholly impertinent tone of voice. If it works for air stewards and teenagers, it might just work for you.

9
Time Off Abroad

*A lovely thing about Christmas is that it's compulsory,
like a thunderstorm, and we all go through it together.*
(Garrison Keillor)

A Yule-ogy to festive flimflam and other frivolities

IN THE BLEAK MID-WINTER

Christmas abroad is almost always a disaster. But then it is
nearly always a disaster at home as well.

A proper family Christmas should involve some opening
salvos over the presents, a few massive broadsides over
lunch, tears and a treaty negotiated over tea, and finally

peace, reconciliation, and a glass of festive spirit over the *Dr Who* special. Everyone then goes home happy and fat, having given their festering sores a Yuletide airing.

The trouble with Christmas abroad is that you either have no family there to score points off, which is no fun at all; or you have the whole lot staying for three entire weeks, which is utterly intolerable. Killing someone becomes a reasonable option. Christmas Cluedo: 'It was Cherry in the dining-room with a yard of tinsel and a turkey-baster.'

In fact, I love Christmas. I adore Midnight Mass, twinkling lights, Christmas carols and cold turkey sandwiches. My children will only be allowed to marry people prepared to climb into bed with me on Christmas morning to open their stockings. I love Christmas so much that I insisted on getting married just before Christmas so that we could have 'Hark the Herald Angels Sing' with the descant on our wedding day. While we were still in the wedding-planning stage, I sent Charlie, who was on language training in Taiwan, a telegram: 'DECEMBER. HARK THE HERALD.'

Back came the reply: 'DECEMBER YES, HARK THE HERALD NO.'

I did not hesitate: 'NO HARK THE HERALD, NO CHERRY.'

Nor did Charlie: 'HARK THE HERALD.'

Sorted.

DECK THE HALLS

Europe is the only place that does Christmas properly. Everywhere else simply makes a dog's dinner of it. I remember one Christmas in Cyprus going into a large supermarket in Nicosia which had been filled to the rafters with sparkly, fluffy, made-in-China Christmas crappery. Standing forlornly in front of a display of tacky Christmas baubles was the Irish Ambassadress. Without even turning her head, she said sadly: 'The first year I was here I thought they were hideous. The second year I thought they were better. This year I'm thinking of buying some. It is time I went home to Ireland.'

The longer you stay away, the lower your yuckometer drops. After five years you will be buying plastic, pink, sparkly snowmen, when outside it is 40 degrees centigrade. A friend in Japan bought a crucified Father Christmas, which only goes to show how baffling our religious iconography must be to the Oriental manufacturer trying to celebrate the commercial season. Still, a crucified Easter bunny would have been worse.

Christmas abroad just is not right. It is hot and sticky

and all the carols are sung with Filipino accents. I shall never forget Freddie aged four with tears streaming down her face after going to see Father Christmas in a shopping mall in Hong Kong. 'He didn't look the same,' she sobbed. Popping my head round the side of his grotto I saw the problem. Father Christmas had morphed into a young, very skinny Cantonese gentleman with a slight acne problem, knobbly knees and an accent that made Jackie Chan sound like Brian Sewell.

Abroad even the Christmas trees are all wrong. In Cyprus we had strange wispy pines which looked bare no matter how many decorations you hung on them. These days you can get artificial ones which look almost real, but they just don't cut the mustard. If a tree doesn't cover your carpet with prickly needles and block your vacuum cleaner then what's the point? I did once find a fake one that tempted me sorely. When you walked near it, a sensor triggered two enormous eyes nestling in its branches, which flew open maniacally. 'Hallooo,' a great voice boomed. 'I'm Douglas Fir!'

O COME, ALL YE FAITHFUL

When you are overseas, the most important part of Christmas, going off to church, can also be the strangest. The celebration is the same, the intentions are the same, but their manifestations most definitely are not.

Wherever you are in the world, the local religious beliefs and culture have left their stamp and have moulded Christian services. A little touch of animism here, a soupçon of voodoo there. In England it often seems to be a cross between an Alcoholics Anonymous meeting and the state opening of parliament. But abroad, expect the unexpected.

We once coincided with Orthodox Easter in Jerusalem. It was chaos. Christians of every shape, size and flavour were piling over each other in their desperation to get anointed, blessed or laid on by various hands. They all carried crucifixes of some kind or another; some had opted for the enormous 'could be used for the purpose intended' version; while others had gone for the smaller 'buy one get fifty free' option. Everywhere people were reeling from crosses in the eye. I have never seen so many sweaty long-bearded priests, all dressed for a Rasputin look-alike competition. We eventually made the sanctuary of the Armenian church, which was deserted for some reason, having passed through the

Serbian sector where I witnessed so much wailing and smiting that I found myself looking up to heaven and praying, 'God, if it's anything like this, I'm not coming.'

No, abroad is different and nothing is more different than going to church at Christmas, particularly in Tripoli. For a start, Midnight Mass began at eleven and concluded three and half hours later. No one told us to take sandwiches.

By the time we arrived, the church was packed, mainly with Tripoli's large sub-Saharan African community, some Filipinos and the odd Iraqi Christian. Being fair-weather churchgoers our intention was to slide inconspicuously into the back pews from whence it would have been easy to make our escape if the need arose. Unfortunately, we were spotted by a Maltese priest, who, to our horror, ushered us to reserved seats right at the front.

We tried to insist on sitting in any old pew, but the Catholic Church is nothing if not insistent, and so we were forcibly seated at God's right hand for the duration.

When the varied array of priesthood arrived our hearts sank. It was going to be a long night. There was a veritable smorgasbord of saintliness: the Bishop was Italian, his right-hand man was Maltese; there was a Korean, a Filipino, an Iraqi and an African. Half-way through the service the Copt showed up in all his kit, showered us with Greek and spit, then disappeared (or 'copt out' as Charlie whispered rather loudly).

Each part of the mass was repeated at least six times in

different languages. We had six sermons, six sets of intercessions and innumerable carols. I lost count of the number of linguists who came out of the congregation to give their special bidding prayers. I swear that the Iraqi priest started the service clean-shaven and ended up with a respectable beard.

Being in the front pews we found ourselves surrounded by four different choirs, drawn from the different nations. This was competitive carolling: *Adeste fidelis* to the death. Every time it was the Iraqi choir's turn to sing, the African choir on our right would chunter and mutter, 'Rubbeesh, they are rrrrub-beesh,' rolling their Rs indignantly. 'We should be singin' this one.' The small and rather charming Filipino carol sung with guitar accompaniment merely caused snorts of derision from the large African ladies, who seemed to measure musicality by volume rather than accuracy of pitch. They stamped their feet and rummaged noisily in their handbags to drown out the weedy singing.

In the face of this onslaught, I am ashamed to say that the family pew started to crack. As so often happens in inappropriate moments we got the giggles. It started with the sermon, or rather one of the five. It was now 1.30 in the morning. The Iraqi priest, whose chin was by now bristling, leant over the lectern and appeared to say with great earnestness and emphasis something in Arabic that sounded strangely like 'What a botty!' The Filipino bidding prayer made things worse by pumping out a stream of Tagalog in the middle of which came the words '... Employment Agency ...', accompanied by a shake of a furious fist. But we were finally finished off during the six months it took for everyone to take communion, when an old African man turned back from the altar rail and we saw in large red letters embroidered across his puffer jacket the words 'Fuckin' Freezin'.

As the final carol came to an end, our hearts beat a little faster. We smelt freedom. We were shaking the earth from our trouser-legs and dreaming of home. But we had reckoned without the bishop's party trick, which was to wish us all happy Christmas in the eight languages he spoke plus another eighteen, which presumably members of the congregation had translated for him. We finally got to bed just before four in the morning.

Shorter, but more excruciating, was the Anglican service in Nicosia. My large Bohemian brother-in-law Jim, a writer, had arrived for Christmas with his two daughters both aged under two and his saintly wife Anna. Jim, a big happy man, with shaggy hair and large feet, is nearing fifty, still plays rugby and is a keen – but bad – pianist. There is something of the second row forward in

Jim's approach to the piano, as he permanently stamps on the loud pedal and treats the instrument like the opposing scrum. Our piano sat in the middle of the house, in a large, marble hall on to which all the rooms on both floors looked. No matter where you were, you could not escape from the musical Six Nations.

By Christmas morning we were all understandably feeling a little fragile. Church would make us all relax and calm down, I thought. It started well until a Cypriot in the pew behind set us off by singing all the hymns very loudly, three words behind and several tones apart from everyone else. Things got worse. My small niece, Josephina, took a fancy to the Baby Jesus, and stole him from the Nativity scene. Tucking Our Lord under her arm and seeing a gap on the right wing, she lowered her head and broke for the door. Another child showed interest, but did a poor tackle, was brushed off and started screaming. Josephina, side-stepping the vicar, dummied a church official and with her father's genes really beginning to kick in, she shimmied past the rest of the opposition to score a try on the front steps. The vicar finally retrieved Baby Jesus from an outraged Josephina (who had been going for a conversion) and got his own back by making us all sing 'Happy Birthday, Dear Jesus'. 'Swing Low' would have been far more appropriate.

HOW
TO
SEED A
POMEGRANATE

1. First cut your pomegranate in half.

2. Holding the knife by the blade, whack your pomegranate robustly with the handle.

The harder you hit, the faster they fall.

FIGGY PUDDINGS AND FESTIVE FLIMFLAMMERY

Try as I do to reproduce the Dickensian dream, I always fail. You can occasionally produce the essentials – the turkey, puddings and pies – but you have to work much harder to get them, unless you have had the foresight to bring them out months in advance from home. Sometimes it's easier to accept defeat and just enjoy a tropical feast.

In China we found that turkeys could not be imported because the word was not on the list of agreed imports. The Americans solved this for their Thanksgiving by persuading the relevant official that a turkey was no more than a large Texan chicken, and chicken was, of course, already on the list.

So, abroad, the first ingredient of a successful Christmas lunch is cunning improvisation. The second is to take disappointment philosophically. In Libya one year I spent a happy evening at the kitchen table of a young embassy colleague, chopping and grating industrial quantities of dates and apples in order to make our variation of homemade mincemeat. We intended to take what we needed and sell the remaining jars to nostalgic expats for charity. By the time I left after midnight we had produced approximately eight tons of the stuff, ready to be put in jars after work the next evening. Rich and fruity, and rather solid, we left it in two large preserving pans on her sideboard.

The next day Helen's cleaning lady, having sniffed, poked and wobbled the contents of the pan, decided that it was toxic waste and chucked the whole lot in the bin. I may advocate the philosophical acceptance of disappointment, but it still comes hard.

After improvisation and philosophical acceptance, the third vital quality you will need is fortitude. You will be invited to a myriad of Christmas events. At home people retreat into their families. Abroad, there is something, maybe the heat, that drives everyone into a frenzy of invitation-issuing. You will have forced upon you every conceivable type of Yuletide goodie: American spiced cakes, thick with rubbery green angelica, great yeasty dumplings as indigestible as billiard balls, stale canapés and snot-filled vol-au-vents which explode on your bosom like an early fall of seasonal snow or terminal dandruff, all served up with syrupy mulled wine.

Freddie was once invited to a regimental Christmas dinner in Cyprus where the menu was based on the Twelve Days of Christmas. The next morning the details were fuzzy, but she was able to remember that by the time she had struggled through the Five Gold (greasy fried calamari) Rings, the joke was fading fast.

Actually, all you need to survive Christmas abroad is a good set of friends. I like the sort who insist that you and your household of hangers-on come to their house for

Christmas lunch and just bring the cran-
berry sauce. I advise always keeping a
good stock of it. I have some ridiculous
photographs from Christmases past.
One with all the men wearing the
underpants someone had had made for
them in the Peking Friendship Store on
the outside like Superman. Another of a
Christmas dinner in Cyprus. Jo, the
Defence Attaché's wife, had invited twenty-four of us and
the immaculately arranged table ran the entire length of
her house and was lit by a hundred candles. Meanwhile,
Julia (another friend and an art historian of note) had
made everyone a hat illustrating some aspect of its wearer.
Charlie had a large silver bicycle on his head throughout
dinner, Barney two rugby posts and a ball. Julia's husband
Rob had a pirate galleon in full sail, while the High
Commissioner had two tennis rackets with a ball strung
between them so that when he turned his head, he could
have a rally with himself. His daughter had an intricate
model of the Leaning Tower of Pisa, to represent her love
of Italy. I couldn't keep my hat, a huge golden easel with a
tiny watercolour of a bowl of cherries, as it got broken on
the way to Libya, but I detached the small painting and
will keep that until I'm eventually put out by the dustbins
with all the old wrapping paper and turkey bones.

PANTOS, PARTIES AND PINK FRILLY KNICKERS

Christmas abroad tends to be a time of odd experiences and parties, the more so if you are in a 'hardship' post, where you often have to make your own entertainment. In Peking in the mid eighties there was a feeling of frustration at the endless harassments of life and the illogical restrictions put on foreigners. The Christmas pantomime was the only chance to poke fun at what we went through for the rest of the year. It was a hot ticket. Charlie and I decided to take its production on one year and chose *Peter Pan*, because the parallels with Never Never Land and China seemed so close. The Lost Boys were clearly the foreign business community, the Fairies matched the Cultural Section, the Pirates were the Political Section, who wanted to keep everyone in the dark about the true state of affairs, and Captain Hook was, of course, the biggest villain of them all: the British ambassador.

It was shortly after the French Secret Service had blown up the Greenpeace ship *Rainbow Warrior*, so we made the Crocodile into a French frogman with a ticking 'bombe'. When word of this reached the French ambassador, he forbade his staff from attending. I am happy to say though that at the opening night the curtain went up to reveal the front rows packed out by the French embassy, who cheered and stamped with the best of them.

Tinkerbell was played by Jasper, the head of the British Council, short, rotund and with a noticeable five o'clock shadow. The other fairies, dressed in pink tutus, leotards and frilly pants, came from the press corps, the largest and hairiest men we could find. Our New Zealand choreographer had them doing a worryingly passable dance of the Cygnets from *Swan Lake*. When I took the frilly pink knickers home to wash at the end of the panto, Ayi laundered them, folded them and put them neatly into Charlie's underwear drawer. Rumours about the British Foreign Office had clearly spread more widely than I had presumed.

The arrival of satellite TV threatens to destroy the sense of home-made fun. What is the fun of the male

members of the family beached in front of the television watching yet another football match? One of my favourite memories from Peking is the annual Boxing Day cricket match between the British and Australian embassies on the ice in the middle of the Summer Palace lake. Kevin Rudd, the current Australian *Prime Minister*, then a rosy-cheeked first secretary, used to open the batting. The setting was far more beautiful than Lords, with a backdrop of golden pagodas, dusted with ice and the seventeen-arch bridge surrounded by silent pavilions.

Fielders were fortified by cups of mulled wine. It was always a tough decision as to whether or not to wear skates, which were fast in the outfield, but made it difficult to balance when throwing the ball. The trouble with wearing skates when you were bowling was that you tended to arrive at the wicket before the ball, although if you were really quick you could do the keeper's job as well and stump yourself. The same choice faced the batsmen: stability of shoes or speed between the wickets, although as everyone ended up crashing on to their coccyxes it didn't make much difference either way.

Of course, the Office Christmas Party is not to be missed on any account, and embassy ones are particularly entertaining as they invariably go gloriously wrong.

There have been moments of delight, such as the time a Chinese conjuror produced a large live fish on a rod from between the legs of the Commercial Counsellor's wife.

And moments of horror as when one rather tight ambassador served old mulled wine and cold, left-over sprouts, both of which I avoid on religious grounds. Later we were ordered into the drawing-room to play party games; not my idea of fun, even if it was amusing to hear the ambassador asking a Third Secretary to help him find his marbles.

These days I am older, wiser and ruthless about leaving early. Not so, when we were on our first posting: I felt I had to support my husband's career. One year in Peking I remember that the after-dinner dancing had started. To prevent 'slippage' the ambassador was by the front door, twitching like a robot whose batteries were running low. I sensed a significant omission. Where was Charlie? Someone had seen him sidling off to the lavatory about five minutes before. I suspected that he had smuggled in an old copy of *The Times* and was whiling away the evening with the crossword. I was blowed if I was going to suffer perspiring colleagues, when it was his job which had dragged me thousands of miles from home.

I went into the downstairs loo to find him standing on the seat. This would not be uncommon in China, but my husband is a conventional man in these matters. The little window above the loo was open. 'Charlie,' I hissed loudly. 'What the hell are you doing?'

'I'm getting out of here. Can't stand another minute.'

'You can't just leave,' I squawked. 'What will everyone say? Think of your career.'

As he slithered out of the tiny window and disappeared into the moonlit bushes, Charlie's voice floated back to me, loud and clear over the embassy lawn: 'Fuck my career.'

YEAR-ROUND JOLLITY

A 'Home Entertainment Centre' abroad usually refers to yet another game of Monopoly, or in my house, a ping-pong tournament on the breakfast table (alongside the breakfast). Keeping yourselves amused in the absence of friends, extended family and all things familiar takes effort and ingenuity.

In Peking, the wife of the *New York Times* correspondent and I joined forces to organise a motorized scavenger hunt. This mostly involved the participants roaring up to the gates of the more paranoid embassies in their cars, leaping out and searching for various clues hidden close to their perimeter walls. The Russians were at the top of the list as they were particularly unfriendly, followed closely by the North Koreans who were most ungracious about returning the tennis balls lobbed over their wall during the diplomatic tennis tournament.

Pub quizzes are another popular way to get a motley assortment of people together – although these, despite involving teams from every embassy, seem only ever to be organised by the British. The French go for bridge

No ~ _anyone_ can join.
Anyone with a chauffeur. We don't want parking to become a problem.

THE
INTERNATIONAL
WOMEN'S
CLUB
COMMITTEE
MEMBER

evenings and recherché musical soirées; the Americans go all out for the Big Two – 4th July and Thanksgiving – but then run out of steam, so it's left to the Brits to muster support for summers fetes, pub quizzes and five-a-side football.

We might have been the instigators of the pub quiz moment, but we weren't always very good at the answers. At one quiz evening in Cyprus, Charlie finally exploded: 'For God's sake!' he yelled. 'Can't we have one question that isn't about bloody pop music?'

'Relax,' said the young quiz master soothingly. 'The next round is history.'

Charlie rubbed his hands and smirked. We played our joker.

'Which year did Kylie Minogue have a hit with her single "Do the Locomotion"?'

In Libya, the pub quizzes were held at the Embassy Club on the outskirts of town. Charlie and I used to turn up without a team and assemble one at the last minute from any waifs and strays new to Tripoli. One evening our team included a large man covered in exotic tattoos. Keen as ever to jolly things along, I asked him whether he had got them in the army.

He grunted. I took it as a yes.

'Oh?' I persisted. 'Which regiment?'

He looked at me for a moment. There was a long

silence. 'Not British,' he finally growled, taking a long drag on his cigarette. 'French Foreign Legion. West Africa. Seventeen years. Sniper.'

Well, I simply couldn't buy him enough beers. And every time he said that Enid Blyton wrote *Harry Potter* and that Budapest was the capital of Rumania, I nodded vigorously and told him he was absolutely right.

The biggest diplomatic mistake I ever made was at a quiz in Nicosia, organised by a committee of women from the Anglican Church. I was still smarting from a trouncing in the pop music categories the previous week so, keen to show how hip I really was, I named our team (which included the septuagenarian bishop and his wife), 'Young, Gifted and Black', after the Bob and Marcia song. I'd heard of it, so I presumed that the dignitaries of the Church would have, too. I presumed wrong . . .

10

Cast Abroad

O brave new world,
That has such people in't.
(Miranda, in *The Tempest*)

People I have loved and listened to

So, after twenty-five years as a Trailing Spouse, what, if anything, have I learnt?

Firstly, that the world is smaller than I ever imagined.

That every country has something they do uniquely well, but that nowhere has found all the answers.

Take something from every place and allow it to change your life a little.

Along the way I have found myself dining with a Maltese diplomat called Ivan Terrible. He was small,

charming and I detected no noticeable fondness for decapitation. I have shaken hands with a Chinese oil executive called Wang Ke (pronounced Ker). I have kept a straight face when introduced to a Turk, whose name is pronounced Bollock Basher. I have secretly sympathized with a Chinese nurse at the British Military Hospital in Hong Kong with the surname Kok, who had been given the Western first-name of Ophelia. I have had tea with Rhubarb Nasser, a cup of coffee with Steamy Chu and engaged in long discussions with an Argentinean called Wilhelm Adolf Espinoza about the exact nature of his mother's political and philosophical outlook.

Nor do foreigners necessarily behave in conventional English ways. In Tripoli I am regularly swept off my feet by a charming African ambassador, whose method of greeting is to grasp you in an enormous hug while declaring: 'I worship your capitalist heart! Let me clasp it to my patriotic socialist bosom.'

Any time, Excellency, any time.

Above all, expect the unexpected and understand it. One beautiful, deep-blue early evening in northern Cyprus, while wandering around the back streets of Kyrenia waiting for Charlie to turn up for dinner, I found myself being pursued by a very insistent, well-dressed young Turk, obviously on the hunt for a rich, lonely widow. Finally, in a desperate attempt to dampen his ardour and send him packing, I told him in rather sharp terms to get a grip – I was old enough to be his mother. 'Is okay, is okay,' he answered, smoothly raising one eyebrow. 'I love antiques, always.'

At a party in Tripoli given by some newly arrived British businessmen, I found that I was the only woman present. All their wives and girlfriends had waited in England to see how the work panned out before applying for their visas. Libyans rarely turn up to parties given by Westerners, and certainly not Libyan women, who are never allowed anywhere without a chaperone. In Libya men and women rarely mix and women's emancipation is, in Western terms, in the Dark Ages. I constantly found myself wishing that women would, as Daisy Ashford so aptly put it in *The Young Visiters*, say enough is enough, take 'the bull by the horn' and move matters into our twenty-first century.

But to my delight a ring on the doorbell heralded the arrival of three very beautiful local girls. We all rushed forward to welcome them, bombarding them with questions. Did they live locally? Were they sisters? Where did they work? It was so unusual to have three single women turn up to a private party – any party. The prettiest one stepped forward, held out her hand to me and said in a clear, ringing voice: 'We are sex girls.'

You could have cut the silence with a chainsaw – a knife wouldn't have been up to the job. The round-eyed businessmen looked panicky, their eyebrows disappearing into their hairlines. I, on the other hand, found myself shaking her hand enthusiastically and saying 'Well done!', like a large lesbian headmistress or a well-trained defence attaché.

Encouraged by my evident approval, she carried on in her beautiful purring Arabic accent, 'Yes, we are sex girls and three boys – quite a big family, I think.'

Definitely, you should expect the unexpected.

AWED ABROAD

Consider this, as you sit in floods of tears on your packing cases: you will meet the most extraordinary people in extraordinary circumstances if you live abroad. Among the weird and wonderful who wandered across my path were George Melly and Luciano Pavarotti. Both these musical mountains came to China.

George Melly was enticed to the British embassy ball one autumn equinox. I was supposed to help keep an eye on him until the ball was over and see him safely back on the aeroplane. This was no mean task: he was like a cross between a rogue rhino and a very tipsy Great Aunt Augusta, a mixture of outrageous campness and butchdom, this a time when China was still highly conservative.

One evening we bussed him and the members of his band, George Chisholm and the Foot Stompers, out to an old Chinese villa on the edge of the Summer Palace. We stoked up George's story-telling and then sat back as he regaled us with scandalously filthy stories, while the great red communist sun slowly sank behind the Fragrant Hills.

As the evening progressed we introduced Mr Melly to the subtle flavours and stimulating robustness of Three-Penis Wine, famous for its restorative qualities. For the intellectually curious, deer, dog and seal contribute their pizzles to this concoction. To my hazy recollection, he drank the entire bottle, while we waited to see if the wine's legendary aphrodisiac properties kicked in. Nothing happened beyond the sinking of the sun and the graceful disappearance below the horizon of the table of those who could not keep up with George.

At the ball, he consumed four bottles of champagne on his own and gave us in return pure joy. We stomped and gyrated to his music, his growling voice like a cement-mixer gargling with gravel. Throughout the night he rumbled out endless jazz classics, covering the proceedings with a decadent glamour – something missing in the humourless communist drabness which blanketed China at that time. I was wearing a gold lamé Mao suit, which I'd had made especially for the occasion, with a matching cap emblazoned with a large red and gold Mao badge. George Melly loved it, but the ambassador told me to go home and change. We compromised by removing the badge from the cap and rolling up the sleeves.

A few years later I was coming out of London's Bibendum restaurant when I bumped into Mr Melly coming in through the same door. I waved and said 'hello'. He looked at me from under the brim of his large floppy fedora, surveyed me for a moment and said in his great booming voice: 'Who the fuck are you?'

I was just about to say, 'Sunset, Summer Palace, Peking,

Three-Penis Wine,' but realized that he could never have remembered any of it.

The second musical legend to cross my path was the not insubstantial Luciano Pavarotti. He arrived in Peking with the Genoa Opera Company, some prize-winning American opera singers and a large television crew in order to stage performances of *La Bohème*. Pavarotti was singing Rodolfo, while the Americans took the other main solo parts and the Chinese opera students from the Peking Academy of Music filled in the smaller roles.

All went swimmingly well until rehearsals for the street scene began. Pavarotti, who was directing as well as performing, wanted a little background colour in the form of a prostitute strutting around behind him, behaving lewdly and getting thrown out of a bar. The Chinese students would not touch the part with a bargepole. Back then, prostitution in China was a relic of the bad old pre-communist days and no one would dishonour themselves by taking the part. The call went out for a Parisian slapper. For some reason the British Embassy was the first place to look. Did we have anyone prepared to behave like an old whore for a week? How could I refuse?

For five nights I got to tart about behind the great man, stick out my bosom, have my face slapped, and get thrown out of a bar. The whole effect was completely ruined by the Chinese music student playing the bar owner: every

Och, go on then...
just a wee one.

THE
HEAD
OF THE
CALEDONIAN
SOCIETY

night after throwing me to the floor, he would rush over to check that I was all right, apologizing profusely.

Watching the hierarchical shenanigans going on inside an Italian opera company was more fascinating than watching Pavarotti himself. The Maestro was, of course, God. Under him came the opera director, then the soloists, followed by the musicians, the wardrobe mistress and finally the technicians. Observing the twisted, mean machinations of this vicious pecking order, I realized that Dante was alive and well and living in Genoa.

Nothing will ever beat the joy of standing in the wings listening to Pavarotti singing. His voice filled the theatre with a sound you could almost hold in your hands. Before leaving China, he gave a concert in the Great Hall of the People, which was one of the most thrilling events I have ever witnessed. He held the 10,000 Chinese spellbound. The Chinese, who would talk incessantly and loudly through any other artistic performance, sat in silence, erupting at the end into deafening foot-stomping applause and chants of '*Pa La Lor Ti, Pa La Lor Ti*', bringing him back for encore after encore, until he finally gave up, exhausted.

FLOORED ABROAD

Finding the unexpected is one of my greatest joys, and people are usually the greatest source of these surprises.

Poke around a bit outside your normal hunting grounds and you'll be amazed at what you find.

After the Israeli bombing of the Lebanon in 2006, Barnaby and I volunteered to go and help with the influx of refugees, who were arriving daily at the docks in Cyprus. As we were expecting to mop floors and help carry suitcases, it was with some trepidation that I found myself seated at a desk processing those who wanted to travel on to the UK. Some clearly knew their minds. One lady had apparently made her way to the Royal Navy ship as it pulled alongside in Beirut and asked to be shown to her cabin, while another had asked if the ship would wait until she had finished her hair appointment. Most, however, were lost and bewildered.

After an hour or so I was beginning to get the hang of it and we were all cracking along at a fine pace. Then up to my desk came an Arab family. He was heavily five o'clock shadowed, with a Village People moustache and a badly fitting suit. She was silent, morose and hijabbed, with two small girls peeking out shyly from behind her long skirts.

The father spoke no English or French, only Arabic. He was tired, grumpy and completely unable to understand my miming skills, which up to then had worked perfectly. We struggled in vain for twenty minutes. Finally, in desperation, he returned to his suitcases to dig out some paperwork which he thought might be useful. The moment he left the table, his wife pushed back her black head-covering, slumped across the desk with her head in her hands and, in a voice *plein de* Thames Estuary, said, 'I dunno why I married that dick.'

My jaw dropped. 'You've been sitting there watching me struggle for half an hour and all the time you're English. Where are you from?'

'Basildon,' she answered sulkily.

I once volunteered to teach on a children's education course run by the UN. While being interviewed by the tiny chic French powerhouse who was in charge, I was asked whether I understood the magnitude of the task. 'Most of the children won't speak English,' she said in her exquisite French accent, 'and most of them won't know what is expected of them. Some of them will have no ideas to give you at all, and will be unable to work on their own. What will you do with those children?'

'Don't worry,' I replied breezily. 'I've taught for years in art schools. With those children, I usually come up with an idea for them, and put it to them in such a way that they think that they have done it for themselves.'

She looked at me stonily, with great disapproval. 'How very British,' she said icily.

Still, I too have been caught out. I once said to the Belgian ambassador's wife in Peking that after living in Belgium for some years, I had come to realize that for all their vaunted prowess in the kitchen, the French came second to the Belgians in the quality of their cuisine. Marie looked at me slowly and said, 'You may be right, Cherry. But I am French.' Who would have guessed that a French would marry a Belgian?

HARDLY EVER BORED ABROAD

I cry when I arrive in a new place and I cry when I leave it. How can you put down roots when the carpet is continually being pulled from under your feet? But then I remember all the extraordinary encounters which have led to unexpected friendships and I know that with each one the world shrinks a little.

I think of Charlie outside a mosque in Kashgar, having an earnest conversation with a Uyghur in Chinese about the merits of Saladin versus Richard the Lionheart.

I remember sitting under the stars in the Acacus mountains with our Tuareg guide, not exactly 'quivering together in the yielding, hot sands', as T.E. Lawrence rather filthily puts it, but definitely bonding, as we compared our favourite Victor Hugo novels. True, I've never actually read one, so I was basing my intellectual arguments on Disney's *Hunchback of Notre Dame*, but I did rather well, I think.

And when the children are in full flight, accusing me of being the most embarrassing mother on the planet, they

HOW
TO MAKE A
STORM LANTERN

OUT OF AN OLD PLASTIC

WATER BOTTLE

1.

Cut the bottle
in half around the
middle.

2.

Using a sharp Knife,
cut a cross in the
bottle top.

3.

Invert the top half
of the bottle and push
a candle inside
through the cross
in the lid.

4.

Weight the bottom
half of the bottle
with sand, water
or pebbles.

5.

Wedge the
top half into
the bottom
half.

A
STORM
LANTERN

often remind me of an episode in Egypt to illustrate my unsuitability for parental responsibility.

We were staying for a few nights in the famous old Cataract Hotel in Aswan. Overlooking the Nile, this venerable hotel had accommodated under its roof Winston Churchill and Agatha Christie. On our first night we all dressed smartly and went down to the great domed dining-room for dinner. As I stood there, looking up at the ceiling in the candlelight with my family all around me, I suddenly felt supremely and unutterably happy. I reached out to my son, who was standing next to me, and grasped him by the nape of his neck, gently pulling on his earlobe with the sort of intimacy only a

mother and son can share. After a few moments I happily ran my hand down his back and gave him a large playful pinch on the bottom. Bringing my gaze reluctantly down from the ceiling I realized that Barney, Freddie and Charlie were all standing facing me with looks of complete horror on their faces.

I turned to see that the

buttock happily clasped in my right hand belonged not to my son, but to a strange blonde Dutch woman.

I did not know the Dutch for 'Madam, I am not a predatory bull-dyke, I just thought you were a man', and I am not sure that it would have made the situation any better. So instead I smiled at her as if she were a very, very lucky person and rejoined my family. I always think that it is better to remain completely calm after touching up a stranger.

Rather than a rolling stone, I think of myself as more of a travelling snowball, picking up useless artefacts (why did I ever think I'd need a Chairman Mao alarm clock or a collection of cockroach art?), smatterings of different tongues (I can say 'where is the lavatory?' in eleven different languages) and an impressive selection of exotic ailments (I'll spare you the details). But along the way I've also collected a wealth of extraordinary adventures and a patchwork of loyal friends I wouldn't have missed for the world.

Of course, there are some aspects of living abroad that

will always lie beyond my comprehension – saunas, tofu and circumcision, to name just three – but when I return to Britain I still find myself enthusing to my friends about my life as a foreigner. They are loyal; they pretend interest, but I have done it often enough to recognize the way their eyes glaze over at my tales of typhoons and tarantulas. I know that they secretly believe I bought my West African voodoo fetish earrings at Accessorize. I can see the way they can barely contain their surprise that I do not know that samphire is the new broccoli.

So, as I write this, we are due to move on again. We don't yet know where, or who we shall bump into when we get there. I sometimes feel I can barely keep pace with the world beneath my feet, and that if I stop for even a second, I shall fall off. But as I cling on by my fingertips I know what I'll be thinking: 'Oh, good! Here we go again.'

Acknowledgements

WITH HUGE THANKS TO ~

OFFICIALLY RECOGNISED HUSBAND

Charlie, who signed, snipped and set right.

* * *

OFFSPRING ~ AT LAST COUNT

Freddie and Barnaby: wanderers extraordinaire.

* * *

MY MONSTROUS REGIMENT OF GIRLFRIENDS

Sue Phipps, Tina Colclough, Juliet Lowes,
Anne Fean and Hilary Munro who dragged me
through by my bootlaces.

* * *

Sister & Supporter

Alex Denman – corrector of spells and sentences.

* * *

Publisher & Woman Most Likely To Take A Punt

Kate Parkin – brave woman and friend.

* * *